Coosa

The Ripley P. Bullen Series
Florida Museum of Natural History

Florida A&M University, Tallahassee
Florida Atlantic University, Boca Raton
Florida Gulf Coast University, Fort Myers
Florida International University, Miami
Florida State University, Tallahassee
University of Central Florida, Orlando
University of Florida, Gainesville
University of North Florida, Jacksonville
University of South Florida, Tampa
University of West Florida, Pensacola

University Press of Florida

Gainesville · Tallahassee · Tampa · Boca Raton

Pensacola · Orlando · Miami · Jacksonville · Ft. Myers

Coosa

The Rise and Fall of a Southeastern Mississippian Chiefdom

Marvin T. Smith

Foreword by Jerald T. Milanich

05   04   03   02   01   00   6   5   4   3   2   1

Library of Congress Cataloging-in-Publication Data
Smith, Marvin T.
Coosa: the rise and fall of a Southeastern Mississippian chiefdom /
Marvin T. Smith; foreword by Jerald T. Milanich.
p. cm. — (The Ripley P. Bullen series)
Includes bibliographical references and index.
ISBN 0-8130-1811-0 (alk. paper)
1. Coosa Indians—History. 2. Coosa Indians—Politics and government.
3. Coosa Indians—Government relations. 4. Mississippian culture—
Coosa River Valley (Ga. and Ala.). 5. Chiefdoms—Coosa River Valley
(Ga. and Ala.)—History. 6. Coosa River Valley (Ga. and Ala.)—Social
life and customs. I. Title. II. Series.
E99.C87414 S55 2000
976.1'6—dc21   00-024536

The University Press of Florida is the scholarly publishing agency for
the State University System of Florida, comprising Florida A&M
University, Florida Atlantic University, Florida Gulf Coast University,
Florida International University, Florida State University, University of
Central Florida, University of Florida, University of North Florida,
University of South Florida, and University of West Florida.

University Press of Florida
15 Northwest 15th Street
Gainesville, FL 32611
http://www.upf.com

For three generations of my family

Contents

Figures and Plates

Figures

Color Plates (following page 76)

Foreword

If someone had asked me two decades ago what Coosa was, my answer would have been "a river in Alabama." At that time I did not know that the Coosa River north of Montgomery took its name from perhaps the greatest and largest American Indian political entity to have existed in the precolumbian southeastern United States. When the entrada of Spanish explorer Hernando de Soto marched the length of Coosa in 1540, the members of his army were in awe of what they were seeing. Coosa's rulers and towns, its people's arts and crafts, were extraordinary indeed.

Twenty years ago I was not alone in my ignorance of Coosa, whose territory stretched from eastern Tennessee into central Alabama. Modern recognition of Coosa emerged only when anthropologist Charles Hudson, working in tandem with Marvin T. Smith and other archaeologists, began to reconstruct the social geography of the sixteenth-century Southeast. Which native groups lived where? What were their social and political relationships to one another? Can we find archaeological sites corresponding to their towns? Hudson and his team answered these questions by focusing on the accounts of early Europeans who traveled through the region, people like Hernando de Soto, and by combining those historical sources with archaeological discoveries.

That research cleared away the mists of time, and Coosa emerged to take its rightful place as a major achievement of the southeastern Indians. A number of archaeologists, including Marvin Smith, have continued to study Coosa, its ancestry, and its transformation in the colonial period.

In his well-illustrated volume Marvin Smith presents this new information for the first time. His synthesis is an excellent overview, one that shows how modern scholarship can contribute fresh perspectives on the native societies of the Southeast. Recognition and understanding of Coosa will change for all time the modern world's view of our nation's past and the accomplishments of the American Indians who once lived here.

Jerald T. Milanich
Series Editor

Preface

The idea for this work stemmed from a Summer Institute on Southeastern Indians and Spanish Explorers directed by Charles Hudson and sponsored by the National Endowment for the Humanities. Many of the participants noted that they could not find supplementary readings on southeastern Indians, archaeology, and ethnohistory that they could use in the classroom. This volume attempts to fulfill that need and is intended for both undergraduates and interested laypersons.

The story of the Coosa Indians is one not only of development and decline but also of perseverance. From humble beginnings, the Coosa people developed what was perhaps the largest paramount chiefdom in sixteenth-century southeastern North America, but the arrival of Spanish explorers during the middle of the sixteenth century forever changed their way of life. The introduction of Old World diseases decimated their population, and their social and political order soon crumbled. A series of population movements was set into motion, and eventually their way of life was altered. They occupied a niche in the deerskin market economy and adopted European domesticated plants and animals to their own use.

I have chosen to look at the Coosa Indians from an archaeological perspective. When possible, I have included historical accounts. Obviously, for the prehistoric period, archaeology is the only source of information. When the Spaniards first arrived in Coosa in 1540, some historical documentation became available. However, this source disappeared following the Spaniards' failure to find the wealth they were seeking.

After 1568 Spaniards simply lost interest in the interior, plunging the Coosa Indians into historical darkness. Only the arrival of other literate Europeans in the eighteenth century gives us additional recourse to the written word.

Many archaeologists have tried to link historically known tribal groups in North America with prehistoric archaeological cultures. This methodology is called the direct historical approach. Often these efforts have failed, due in large part to the disruptions caused by European contact. Following contact, Native groups were decimated by disease, starvation (because of disrupted planting and harvesting cycles and the intruders' greed for their stored foods), and outright murder by Europeans. Survivors often regrouped and frequently moved long distances. Intertribal warfare, often accelerated by contact, was also a factor in survival and movements. If disease decimated one group, their traditional enemies often took advantage of this weakness and attacked. For these reasons, it is difficult to work back in time from groups known in the eighteenth and nineteenth centuries.

In Coosa we have an unusual opportunity. Here we have early sixteenth-century Spanish accounts of relatively pristine Mississippian societies that can, I believe, be linked with specific archaeological sites. Given this sixteenth-century baseline, the archaeologist/ethnohistorian can work backward into prehistory as well as forward to connect with the historically documented groups. Elsewhere I have labeled this the "indirect historical approach"—working from the "middle" (the sixteenth century) into historically undocumented periods of prehistory and the seventeenth century (Smith 1987). Thus for Coosa, we have a rare combination of circumstances. We can put together the story of a group of Native Americans from prehistoric times until the well-documented late eighteenth- and early nineteenth-century period.

Coosa stands alone in the Southeast in the completeness of its archaeological record and in that record's agreement with historical and ethnohistorical sources. Only the records of some of the Iroquoian groups of the Northeast rival that of Coosa in eastern North America. For Coosa, we can discuss the evolution of a complex chiefdom, view the effects of European contact on such a system, and document the devolution of the system into tribal societies.

Over the years, several scholars have worked out the archaeology of Coosa. Although initial work in the area goes back to the late nineteenth century, most of the best information has been collected since 1960. This was done by researchers from the University of Georgia, the University of Alabama, and the University of Tennessee. Professors A. R. Kelly and David J. Hally conducted the archaeology of the core of the Coosa chiefdom, the Coosawattee River Valley. Much additional work was done by an interested amateur, James B. Langford. My own participation in this region was as a student and field supervisor (under Hally) at the University of Georgia archaeological field school at the Little Egypt site. Later, I worked as a field assistant to Patrick Garrow and eventually to David Hally at the King site on the Coosa River. Since that time, much of my research has focused on the Indians of the Coosa area. Further collaboration with Charles Hudson and Chester DePratter involved tracing the routes of European explorers in the Southeast. We reconstructed the routes of Hernando de Soto, Tristán de Luna, and Juan Pardo, which did much to aid our understanding of the Coosa Paramount Chiefdom. My doctoral dissertation research examined the effects of Spanish exploration on the Coosa Indians, eventually leading to a book (Smith 1987).

Recently, more work has been done on the Coosa area, and many previously unreported or vaguely reported excavations have been analyzed. I am particularly indebted to the Alabama De Soto Commission for a grant to study the Coosa River collections at Moundville, Alabama. I am also deeply grateful to the University of South Alabama for research release time that allowed me to draft the manuscript for this book. Continuing research in northeast Alabama by Harry Holstein, Keith Little, and Caleb Curren has brought forth new data about the area. Although we often disagree in our interpretations of the data, I am indebted to them for sharing the results of their work in a professional manner.

The emerging picture of Coosa has been a collaborative effort of many scholars. I am particularly indebted to professors Charles Hudson, David Hally, Vernon Knight, Gregory Waselkov, Jeffery Quilter, Marion Rice, Mark Moberg, David Anderson, and an anonymous reviewer for their comments on early drafts of the manuscript. Their insight added much to the project, although I have not always followed their advice. Carey

Oakley and Eugene Futato, of the Alabama Division of Archaeology, have aided my research in many ways. Illustrations not otherwise credited were drafted by my wife, Julie Barnes Smith.

This narrative is one interpretation of the rise and fall of the Paramount Chiefdom of Coosa. I have based it on the best archaeological data available, but like all scientific reconstructions of the past, it is subject to change as new evidence is gathered. For many areas along the Coosa River, the evidence at hand is likely to be all we will ever know. A series of reservoirs has flooded many archaeological sites, but this was not an unmitigated loss. Reservoir construction has stimulated and funded much archaeological research, giving us one of the best-documented major river drainages in the Southeast. In addition to the professional excavations, the Coosa River has been the scene of many amateur investigations over the years. I have used data from collectors, whenever possible, to improve the picture. I am particularly indebted to Juanita Battles, Steve Hunter, Jon Peek, Frank Cooney, Dr. E. M. Lindsey, Patsy Hanvey, the late Jack Greer, and Venice Gober.

Perhaps the most critical assistance in this project was provided by a former student, Larry Davis. Mr. Davis had returned to school following his retirement from the Air Force in order to pursue a writing career. He offered to assist in a total rewrite of my manuscript for nothing more than an acknowledgment. Without his skill with the English language, this project would never have seen the light of day. The manuscript has benefited greatly from his hours of translating my crude prose into readable English. I am greatly indebted to him. Lisa Johns did an outstanding job of final copyediting. Jerald Milanich provided funds for illustrations and indexing through the Archaeology Endowment Fund of the Florida Museum of Natural History.

For some time in the sixteenth century the Coosa Paramount Chiefdom controlled much of eastern Tennessee, but I have chosen to place less emphasis on this area. While sixteenth-century occupations are well known, little research has been conducted on seventeenth-century occupations so the picture is not as complete as we would like. Furthermore, the people who lived on the Tennessee River in the sixteenth century had usually settled with other groups in other regions by the eighteenth century. Therefore, I have chosen to focus on the people who inhabited the Coosa River, especially the Coosa and Abihka peoples.

I have chosen to limit my discussion to the period ca. A.D. 900–1775. The beginning date is the approximate time that Mississippian cultures took shape in the area. The end date is largely arbitrary. This is the period best known by archaeologists. By the 1790s historical documentation far exceeds current archaeological evidence, so at this point the story falls largely to the historians. The area in which the Coosa-Abihka settled in the eighteenth century was always the most remote from Europeans, so we have little documentation for the period before 1775. This forces us to rely on archaeological research, aided by scant historical sources, to present a picture of the era.

This project also chronicles how we have come to know about the Coosa people. A quarter of a century ago, archaeologists had some knowledge of the prehistory of northern Georgia and Alabama. They developed archaeological "cultures," collections of shared characteristics of pottery styles and other artifact types, largely separate from historically known tribes. During the 1960s and 1970s, reservoir construction in the area brought about ever increasing knowledge of the prehistory. Still, archaeologists could not connect the prehistoric occupants of the region with any later documented people. They described individual archaeological sites but made no regional integration of the information. Chapters 1 and 2 discuss the regional environment and prehistory as it was known somewhat separate from historically known people.

By the late 1970s, ethnohistorian Charles Hudson, archaeologist Chester DePratter, and I began working together. We intended to decipher information contained in sixteenth-century historical accounts left by Spanish explorers. An interest in the expedition of Hernando de Soto (1539–1543) rekindled our efforts to connect historically named groups of people with archaeological cultures. A major breakthrough occurred when we studied documents from the slightly later expeditions of Juan Pardo (1566–1568). Pardo traveled along much of the same route that de Soto had followed twenty-five years earlier, but the documentation of Pardo's route was much better and allowed us to reconstruct it on modern maps. With this reconstruction of Pardo's route, a large segment of the de Soto route became known. Finally, we reconstructed the 1559–1560 expedition of Tristán de Luna into much of the same area, gathering more valuable information. Chapter 3 describes this research.

Working from the other end of the time scale, ethnohistorians, archaeologists, and historians had for years assembled information on the southeastern Indians of the eighteenth and nineteenth centuries. This information did not tie into the earlier prehistory in any real manner. It only noted that the descriptions of the people of the eighteenth and nineteenth centuries were vastly different from the descriptions left by the Spanish explorers. Some researchers assumed that sixteenth-century groups lived in the same areas as their eighteenth-century descendants. Thus, the town of Coosa described in sixteenth- and eighteenth-century accounts was assumed to be the same place for years (Swanton 1939). Only when the site was finally excavated did it become clear there was no sixteenth-century occupation at the eighteenth-century location (DeJarnette and Hansen 1960). There was little effort to correlate prehistoric cultures with historically documented groups in an objective, scientific manner. Chapter 4 details what we know of the eighteenth-century Upper Creek Indians, a people we now know descended from the prehistoric occupants of the northern Georgia–northern Alabama area.

Chapter 5 describes the historical reconstruction of the sixteenth-century Paramount Chiefdom of Coosa. It was accomplished using information contained in the sixteenth-century Spanish accounts and the archaeological data. Coosa is one of the most interesting complex chiefdoms documented in North America, or elsewhere for that matter. It was a large, complex political organization that encompassed thousands of people speaking several different languages. Without the benefit of the Spanish documents, its existence would never have been suspected. Its reconstruction constitutes an excellent example of the power of historical archaeology—that is, research that combines patterned material remains recovered by archaeologists with information available to historians and ethnohistorians through documentary research.

Thus evolved a basic understanding of Coosa of the sixteenth century and the Upper Creeks, including the town of Coosa, of the eighteenth century. What was lacking was an understanding of how the powerful and complex chiefdom of Coosa degenerated into a weak tribal society in the eighteenth century. This story, in chapter 6, "The Lost Years," proposes an account of the collapse of the sixteenth-century chiefdom and its transformation into the eighteenth-century society. Without literate Europeans in the interior in the period ca. 1568–1675, this story must be told through archaeology. It remains the final large piece of the puzzle.

Chapter 7 summarizes the story of the Coosa people as we now understand it. Here I discuss some conclusions and make suggestions for future research.

This story was originally designed to be a popular work, bringing the story of the Coosa people to a lay readership. It is not a theoretical treatise but is intended to be a readable account of the story of the Coosa people according to my interpretations of historical and archaeological data. I hope it will be read with that in mind.

1

Prehistory of the Coosa Area to A.D. 900

Coosa was one of the largest Native American nations visited by six-teenth-century Spanish explorers. In this volume I use the name *Coosa* in three senses: for the *town of Coosa,* which moved to several locations through time; to refer to the prehistoric and sixteenth-century *chiefdom of Coosa,* which was limited to the Coosawattee River Valley in prehis-tory and known to Spaniards as the Province of Coosa; and for the *Paramount Chiefdom of Coosa,* an alliance of several chiefdoms from eastern Tennessee to central Alabama under leadership of the Coosa chief. The Hernando de Soto expedition visited portions of this territory in 1540. A detachment of the Tristán de Luna expedition of 1560 also visited Coosa. Finally, the Juan Pardo expedition of 1567–1568 explored the area. Each explorer described the Province of Coosa as consisting of several separate towns. By combining information from all three expe-ditions, we know that the Coosa Paramount Chiefdom stretched for a distance of some four hundred miles. Its capital was at the Little Egypt archaeological site on the Coosawattee River in northwest Georgia (Hud-son et al. 1985) (fig. 1). (See chapter 5 for more discussion of the identi-fication of this area as Coosa.)

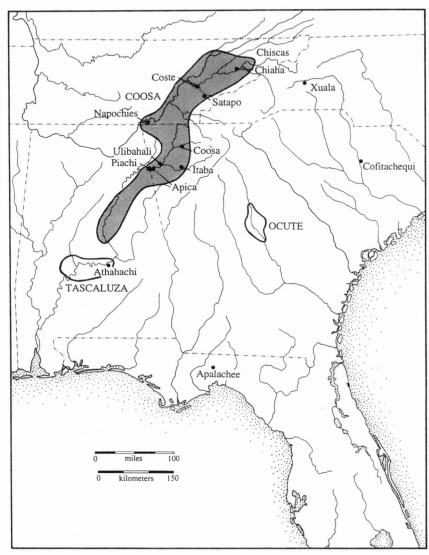

1. The Paramount Chiefdom of Coosa. Map by Julie Barnes Smith.

To examine the genesis, rise, and decline of the Coosa people from the period A.D. 900 to 1775, we must rely on several fields of study. These include prehistoric archaeology and historical sources such as those left by early Spanish explorers. After the mid-sixteenth century, we must rely on historical archaeology (that is, archaeology that benefits from some historic accounts or datable European artifacts). Finally, we must use historic accounts left us by English and French explorers and traders of the eighteenth century. Thus, this volume is a multidisciplinary exercise. It combines archaeology, ethnohistory, and history to piece together the story of the Coosa people.

Coosa apparently began as a small, simple chiefdom located in northern Georgia. Later it expanded, and by the sixteenth century it encompassed settlements in much of the upper Tennessee and Coosa River drainages. This area includes eastern Tennessee and the northern halves of Georgia and Alabama. Following European contact, the people of Coosa fragmented and declined as European disease took its toll. They migrated and eventually became a part of the Creek Confederacy of the eighteenth century. Before tackling the full story, however, we must understand the setting.

Introduction to the Ridge and Valley Province

Even at its height as a paramount chiefdom, Coosa was confined to an area geologists and geographers call the Ridge and Valley Province (see fig. 2). This area is a broad band of sedimentary rock that follows the western border of the Appalachian Mountains from New York to Alabama. Geologic activity has folded and faulted these rocks. Erosion has left a terrain consisting of parallel ridges and valleys running from northeast to southwest. These ridges make east-west travel difficult, and the rivers that cut through them provide the only passage, thus making it likely that water travel was essential to the east-west travel axis.

Streams in the Ridge and Valley Province flow from the foothills of the Appalachian Mountains toward the southwest. They form the Tennessee River drainage and the Coosa-Alabama River drainage. Major streams in the study area include (from north to south), the French Broad, Little Tennessee, and Hiwassee Rivers of the Tennessee River system and the Conasauga, Coosawattee, Oostanaula, and Etowah, which form the

Coosa-Alabama River system. The Tennessee River system flows into the Ohio River, then to the Mississippi River and the Gulf of Mexico. The Coosa River joins with the Tallapoosa River to form the Alabama River, which eventually flows into Mobile Bay on the Gulf. These river systems were rich in fish and shellfish, and the Native Americans frequently exploited these species. The riverbanks provided rich alluvial soil that was easily tilled by primitive methods. Agriculture provided corn, beans, squash, sunflowers, and other seeds as food sources.

The forest cover of the Ridge and Valley is classified as oak-pine and oak-hickory-pine (Braun 1950; Kuchler 1964). Dominant species include white oak, black oak, red oak, and southern red oak, white hickory, pignut hickory, and shortleaf and loblolly pine. The rich environment supports many animals, including deer, bear, raccoon, opossum, and wild turkey. These are the species most commonly hunted by Native Americans. Many wild nuts, seeds, and fruits also occur in this environment, adding to the variety of foods available to Native Americans and their animal prey.

The climate of the Georgia portion of the Ridge and Valley Province is moderate. The rainy season occurs between December and March. Annual rainfall ranges from 50 to 65 inches (1270–1651 mm). There are about 215 frost-free days per year, more than in the adjacent Blue Ridge or Piedmont provinces. The longer growing season is one reason that Native Americans chose to locate their towns in the Ridge and Valley.

Many of the larger towns of the Coosa Paramount Chiefdom were located on the border between two different environmental zones. Geographers and ecologists call this type of area an ecotone. Coosa lay between the Ridge and Valley and other physiographic provinces. In Georgia and Alabama, the ecotone boundary is the Piedmont physiographic zone. In eastern Tennessee and extreme northern Georgia, the boundary is the Blue Ridge physiographic province. This geographical border location of the towns allowed the inhabitants to use the resources of two very different areas (Larson 1971a). The ecotone boundary also served as a geological break point, or fall line, of the rivers flowing to the west. Often shoals were present, providing good fishing resources and an easy place to cross the streams for north-south travel. The locations of these crossings formed the Great Indian Warpath, an important historic Indian trail

(Myer 1928). These shoal locations also marked sudden changes in stream gradient. As the streams fell from the more mountainous Blue Ridge and Piedmont provinces, they deposited alluvial soils at the base of the mountains. Rich in minerals, these small pockets of soil suitable for primitive cultivation were another strong attraction for the Indians (Hally, Smith, and Langford 1990). To understand the importance of the ecotone location of the Coosa Paramount Chiefdom, we must first understand the nature of the adjoining Piedmont and Blue Ridge physiographic provinces.

To the east of the Ridge and Valley, the Piedmont is dominated by rolling hills of metamorphic rocks. The present vegetation consists of hickory, shortleaf and loblolly pine, and white and post oak species. The Piedmont can be seen as a transitional forest zone between the Blue Ridge, which is dominated by oak and chestnut, and the longleaf pine forests of the Coastal Plain (Larson 1971a:23–24). The Piedmont produces many types of stone used by Native Americans: graphite, galena, greenstone, soapstone, and ochre. It provided stone suitable for ground stone axes and other tools, while the Ridge and Valley contained rocks suitable for the production of flaked stone tools (Larson 1971a:25).

The Blue Ridge Province is a more mountainous area of metamorphic rock that includes the Appalachian chain. This area is primarily oak-chestnut forest, again an area rich in nuts and therefore in wildlife. Mountain soils are thin but well drained. Climates in the Blue Ridge are moderate. The Blue Ridge also provided raw material for ground stone tools and soft soapstone for carving pipes and ornaments. It also produced copper, an important trade item in the prehistoric period (Wynn 1990).

This rich ecotone environment supported major populations of Indians in the prehistoric and historic periods. The many wild resources, coupled with native agriculture, provided a stable existence for the Coosa people. They found this region so bountiful in the resources they needed to survive and prosper that they inhabited the area for hundreds of years. However, as for many Indians in the eastern woodlands, European contact brought great changes in their lives. The Coosa people nevertheless managed to remain in their Ridge and Valley environment until the nineteenth century. Then forced removal by Euroamericans relocated them to present-day Oklahoma.

Pre-Mississippian Archaeology

Before discussing Coosa, we must review the prehistory of the area that later became the core of the paramount chiefdom. The early story of Coosa focuses on northern Georgia before Coosa's expansion, so this discussion will focus on what we know of northwest Georgia prehistory. Most generalizations, however, will include the total area later controlled by the Coosa Paramount Chiefdom in the sixteenth century. The center of focus will be the Coosawattee River Valley, the location of the chiefdom of Coosa (fig. 2).

There is good evidence that people first occupied northern Georgia during the Paleoindian period, circa 13,500–10,000 B.C. (Fiedel 1999). Paleoindians were hunters and gatherers, a nomadic people who moved around seeking food resources. In the western United States, Paleoindian archaeological sites document the use of now-extinct animals, such as mastodons and some species of bison. Evidence of the use of such large animals in the Southeast is scarce, although we do have a report for northern Florida (Webb et al. 1984). It is possible that eastern Paleoindians relied on smaller mammals, such as deer.

The Pleistocene, or ice age, was a time of much cooler climate, even in the Southeast. Glaciers covered much of Canada and the present Great Lakes area. Boreal forest and tundra environments characterized much of the northern half of the present United States, and large herd animals roamed in these environments. Archaeologists have characterized Paleoindians as "big game hunters." However, it is likely that they also hunted smaller game and relied on wild vegetable foods such as nuts, seeds, and fruits.

Paleoindians lived in small groups, probably bands of fifty people or less. Such groups are usually related by blood or by marriage. Each band probably recognized its own hunting territory, but an overall low population density probably made disputes over territory rare. The presence of distinctive stone tools, especially projectile points, marks Paleoindian archaeological sites. The earliest point style is Clovis, named for a town in New Mexico near one of the first finds. Clovis points are long, lanceolate projectile points with distinctive flutes. These flutes are long thinning grooves running up from the base to aid in attaching the point to a wooden or bone shaft (fig. 3). Clovis points were probably used on spears

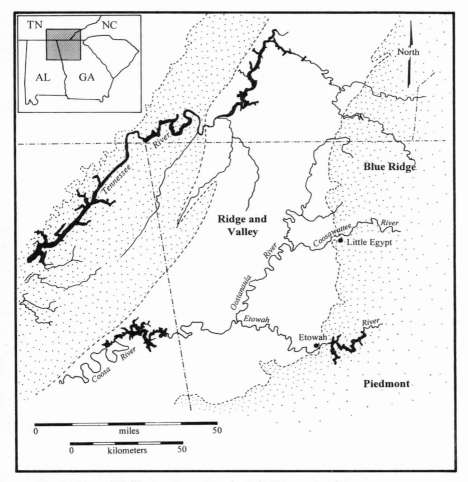

2. The Ridge and Valley Province. Map by Julie Barnes Smith.

that were held and thrust into large game animals or propelled by a throwing stick, or atlatl.

Later Paleoindian occupations are known by slightly different projectile-point styles. Quad points are basically unfluted Clovis points with ears projecting from the basal corners. Related Dalton points are often resharpened, resulting in a steeply beveled appearance. Through time, projectile points diminished in size, probably as the climate changed and the large Pleistocene animals became extinct.

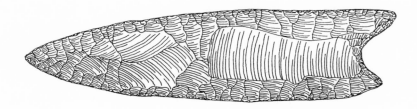

3. Clovis point. Drawing courtesy of Jerald Ledbetter.

Artifacts of the Paleoindian period have been found in several counties of northwest Georgia, but none has been recovered from the Coosa-wattee River drainage (Anderson, Ledbetter, and O'Steen 1990). Certainly, Paleoindians were present in the study area, as further research will undoubtedly confirm. The low population density of Paleoindians and the fact that alluviation has buried early sites in the Coosawattee Valley make such occupations hard to locate.

Following the Paleoindian era is the period known as the Archaic, circa 10,000–3,000 B.P. This was a period of changing adaptations to the modern environment. As the Pleistocene herd animals became extinct, hunting patterns were adapted to solitary forest animals, such as deer. Modern forests evolved during this period, and the Archaic peoples developed patterns of seasonal use of natural resources.

During the Archaic, people gradually became more sedentary. They lived in one place for longer periods instead of leading a strictly nomadic existence. In some parts of the Southeast they even learned to grow a few domesticated plant species toward the end of the period: squash, gourds, sunflowers, and starchy seeds, such as sumpweed and chenopodium (B. Smith 1989). Although there is no evidence of the use of domesticated plants in northwest Georgia, it is likely that further archaeological research will prove their use.

The Indians also adapted their technology to the changing environment. As modern forests emerged, tools for woodworking became more important. Ground stone tool technology was used to manufacture axes, adzes, and other tools. Smaller animals required smaller projectile points, and point styles changed over the several thousand years of the Archaic. When found in contexts allowing radiocarbon dating, these changing styles aid in the construction of a detailed chronology of the Archaic. The stone-tipped dart replaced the thrusting lance of the Paleoindian period. The dart was hurled by an atlatl, or spear thrower. The atlatl itself required many parts. These included a hook, often of antler or bone, a wooden shaft, sometimes an antler or bone handle, perhaps even a stone weight (bannerstone) to add force to the throw.

Populations steadily increased during the Archaic. By the end of the period, some groups in the Southeast had evolved a way of life that enabled them to settle into a more sedentary existence. Large shell middens (heaps of discarded river mussel shells) reflect the continued occupation of many places on major rivers in the Southeast. Such shell heaps are found along the Tennessee River in Tennessee and Alabama and on the Savannah River in Georgia, although they are not known in northwest Georgia.

This new lifestyle provided a stable economic basis. As certain Archaic people settled into it, they had time to develop other aspects of their culture. They invented pottery late in the Archaic. The earliest examples known are from the Savannah River drainage of Georgia and South Carolina. This early pottery is known as fiber-tempered pottery because of the addition of vegetable fibers to the clay to prevent it from cracking during drying. Fiber-tempered pottery has been found in many areas of the Southeast, even in places where there is not particularly good evidence for a sedentary lifestyle. Although rare, fiber-tempered pottery has been found on the Coosawattee drainage. In some areas of the Southeast, soapstone was carved into bowls in the late Archaic, further evidence of the "container revolution" (Smith 1986:28) that took place with increased sedentism. It also marks the beginnings of long-term food storage and perhaps new cooking techniques. Soapstone bowl fragments have also been found in the Coosawattee Valley, at site 9Mu104 (fig. 4) (Kelly 1976).

The Woodland period, 1000 B.C. to A.D. 900, provides the first definite evidence of a sedentary lifestyle in northwest Georgia. Small communities of several households grew up, particularly along the river bottoms. Pottery, typically tempered with sand or crushed limestone, was in daily use, and archaeological sites of the Woodland period often yield hundreds or even thousands of fragments. These sites contain evidence of round or oval houses of individually set posts. Intentional human burials, deep

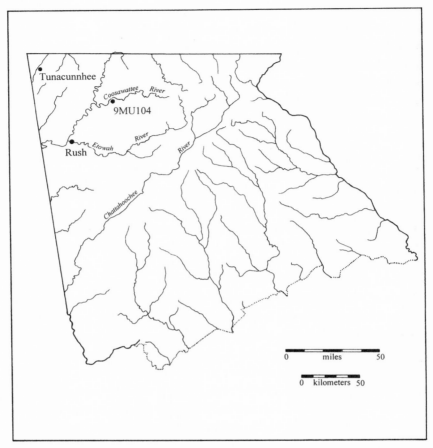

4. Pre-Mississippian archaeological sites. Map by Julie Barnes Smith.

storage pits often filled with acorns or hickory nuts, and other evidence of an increasingly sedentary lifestyle have also been found (Caldwell 1958).

By the middle of the Woodland period, emphasis shifted from hunting and gathering to greater reliance on domesticated plants. Although some corn (maize, introduced from Mexico) may have been present in the Woodland period, it does not appear to have been of any real economic importance. What was important was the use of native eastern North American plants. Chenopodium, sumpweed, sunflower, knotweed, maygrass, and little barley were grown for their seeds. Their yields per acre rivaled that of maize or wheat (B. Smith 1989:1569). This is not to say that wild plants or meat from hunting and fishing were no longer a major portion of the diet. The new horticulture simply added to an already rich subsistence base. On this basis, populations grew.

Within the Coosawattee Valley, there is evidence of several different Woodland period occupations, but they have not been thoroughly investigated. At site 9Mu104, three types of pottery were recovered in an area being bulldozed for reservoir construction: Early Woodland fabric-marked pottery, Middle Woodland Cartersville check-stamped pottery, and Middle to Late Woodland Swift Creek complicated stamped pottery (Kelly 1976). These remains indicate occupation, perhaps intermittently, over several hundred years during the Woodland period. Evidence for domesticated plants is lacking for this area, primarily because of lack of research, but recent excavations have yielded corn in a Woodland context at the Rush site in nearby Floyd County (fig. 4) in northwest Georgia (Wood and Ledbetter 1990:136–38).

When people remained in one place, archaeologists have a better chance of finding artifacts not oriented to subsistence. These materials give us a better view of their social and religious lifestyles. By the Middle Woodland period, there is evidence of the beginnings of social inequality. Some people enjoyed a higher status than others and were buried in earthen burial mounds, sometimes with elaborate offerings. This is the time of the Hopewellian Interaction Sphere (Caldwell 1964), a long-distance elite trade network that connected groups of people from Montana to the Great Lakes to Florida. There was trade in many exotic goods, among them copper from the Great Lakes area and eastern Tennessee and marine shells, shark teeth, and stingray spines from the Gulf Coast. Mica came from the Appalachian Mountains and galena (lead ore used as a pigment) from Missouri. Silver came from the Great Lakes, obsidian from the Rocky Mountains. Fancy decorated pottery came from many areas.

The tribal leaders of the society were often buried in elaborate tombs with log or stone linings, placed in or under conical earthen mounds. Finely crafted items were placed in the tombs as grave goods. These included carved stone pipes, axes, pottery vessels (presumably containing some perishable substance, perhaps a food offering), and fancy ornaments of copper and mica. In northwest Georgia, the Tunacunnhee site (Jefferies 1976) is a good example of this phenomenon (fig. 4). Tunacunnhee consists of four burial mounds and a nearby village area. Burials included such artifacts as copper earspools, breastplates, and panpipes; stone axes, knives, and pipes; mica cutouts; and pottery vessels. It is possible that the Tunacunnhee inhabitants controlled trade in copper or mica from the Tennessee, North Carolina, and Georgia area. They may also have acted as middlemen for other goods.

Anthropologist Bruce Smith (1986) suggests that these societies were of the "Big Man" type—a society led by a male who has what is known as "achieved status." He becomes wealthy by hard work, favorable marriage ties, and good trading. Over time he has gained a leadership position by his own hard work and influence over others. Big Man societies are not particularly stable. At the death of the Big Man there was no mechanism for succession, and a new leader had to rise and take over. The Big Man societies of the Middle Woodland period show an increasing social complexity, but they were far different from the type of organization that was to come in the Mississippian period.

The Late Woodland period in the immediate study area is poorly known. From a larger perspective of northwest Georgia, there is evidence of a Hamilton-like culture better known from eastern Tennessee (Lewis and Kneberg 1946). There is also some evidence of the poorly known Napier Culture (Wauchope 1966). The region does not appear to have been abandoned, but little is known of the Late Woodland lifestyle.

From the rather poorly known Paleoindian, Archaic, and Woodland occupations of northwest Georgia, we may now turn to the much better documented Mississippian cultures of the region. Here the real story of the Coosa people begins.

2

Coosa after A.D. 900
The Mississippian Period

Following the Woodland period, archaeologists recognize a final prehistoric period in the study area: the Mississippian period, A.D. 900–1540. Mississippian people are believed to be the direct descendants of local Late Woodland peoples. They emphasized cultivated plants, especially corn, beans (a new addition to the diet), and squash. Woodland period domesticated plants continued to be grown for their nutritious seeds. Cultivated plants became a major portion of the diet, and new plants continued to be added to the diet well into the historic period. Explorers and colonists introduced plants from Europe, Asia, and Africa. Hunting and fishing were still the only source of meat protein, but hunting technology improved with the introduction of the bow and arrow, probably in the Late Woodland period. Again, an increase in the subsistence base led to a growth in population. Mississippian town sites became much larger and more impressive than their Woodland village forebears.

There was a basic reorganization in social and political structure. A ranked society, or chiefdom form of government, emerged in most areas of the Southeast. A chiefdom has a system of ascribed status, whereby one is born into a certain social position. Here is the beginning of hereditary leadership. Chiefs and nobles are distinguished from commoners, and the chief is the highest ranking member of society, the person who can prove the closest genealogical link to the founding ancestors of the society, who are often mythical beings. Close blood relatives of the chief have a slightly lower rank. Some great warriors achieved exalted status because of their feats. There were also commoners and in some cases slaves, who were usually war captives.

Vernon Knight (1990) has carefully analyzed the sociopolitical system of southeastern Indians. The following discussion is based on his analysis. Southeastern Indians had exogamous clans that functioned in marriage, hospitality, and settlement of disputes. Within the clans, there was no social ranking. Everyone within a clan was essentially equal.

The clans were divided into two opposing groups, which in some cases were exogamous (true moieties). These were always ritual groups, often associated with war and peace. Of key importance, according to Knight, is the "ingrained notion of hierarchy," that "one group was believed to be superior to the other" (Knight 1990:6). In some cases, in addition to the dual divisions, the actual clans were ranked. It is from this system of clan ranking that one group became in essence a royal family and ruled the Mississippian chiefdoms.

Kinship in the Southeast was matrilineal, and the office of chief and other specific offices were inherited through the mother. Usually the chief's sister's eldest son (or, rarely, daughter) became chief, while her other sons and sons of other females in the ruling matrilineage inherited other high-status positions. Knight believes, however, that certain high-status positions were inherited through the male line. Thus the children (or perhaps only the sons) of chiefs retained their nobility, instead of reverting to the commoner status of their mothers, who had to be commoners since the "royal" matrilineage was exogamous. Strictly speaking, these children belonged to the clans of their mothers but retained aristocratic status inherited from their royal fathers, and thus many other clans had this level of aristocracy. Thus, in practice "royalty" was not limited to a single clan but rather crosscut clans and thus served to link them together into society. Potentially any clan could have an aristocrat if one of its female members married someone in the ranking (ruling) clan. Knight also believes that, beyond a specified degree of genealogical distance from the royal line, the agnatic aristocracy would revert to commoner status. Male children of male nobles inherited a noble status of lesser rank than their father, instead of inheriting the commoner status of their mother. "Noble status degenerated by grades in the male line, and was limited to a specified number of generations" (Knight 1990:19). In this way most if not all clans had links to the royal clan, yet since the statuses degenerated by generation, few people in any given clan could claim noble status.

Power was inherited. The main office of chief remained in the royal clan, but lesser levels of royalty spread to other clans via marriage ties through the agnatic system of inheritance of high status. Genealogy was important but primarily only in the ruling clan and perhaps only for a specified number of generations. Beyond these limits, all people were commoners.

Archaeological evidence of such social ranking can be seen in the types, quantities, and location of graves and grave goods (Peebles and Kus 1977). The elite segment of society is usually buried in a special location. In the present study area, elite burials are placed in mortuary temples built atop earthen mounds. The elite were also often buried in special graves, such as log-lined tombs or stone box graves. Frequently, markers of elite status accompany these burials: flint swords and ornaments hammered out of native copper or carved from marine shells, and special forms of axes, fine textiles, and exotic pottery vessels traded over long distances (see plate 1).

For the first time in our study area, there was multiple-town political organization. Chiefdoms usually have a capital town, and several subsidiary towns pay tribute to the chief. The chief controls food surpluses, which he or she uses for various purposes. These include feasting, supporting part-time artisans who make special goods for the elite, and supporting the warriors. Many chiefdoms around the world are known to have been very warlike, and Mississippian chiefdoms of the Southeast were no exception. Since prowess in war enabled some low-ranking people to join the ranks of the elite, this was, in fact, the main avenue to elevated status. Prehistoric art from the Southeast is rich with themes associated with war, illustrating the warlike nature of the chiefdoms (Brown 1976). The reports of Hernando de Soto's expedition bear witness to this fact. Early Spanish accounts describe warriors arranged in complex formations of squadrons and flotillas of war canoes.

According to one archaeological model, simple chiefdoms consist of a cluster of towns or villages with a capital town (Steponaitis 1978). Usually surrounding the chiefdom is a buffer zone of unoccupied lands that protected it from its enemies and served as a hunting preserve. A typical town of the mid-sixteenth century in the present study area consisted of forty to sixty households with a total population of around five hundred people. The chiefdom probably consisted of five to eight such towns. Coosa started as such a simple chiefdom but later became more complex.

A complex chiefdom has more than one tier of administrative centers (Steponaitis 1978). Typically there would be a capital, one or more secondary administrative centers, other towns, and in some cases hamlets and isolated farmsteads. However, these latter two site types are rare in our study area. Such hierarchies are often visible in the archaeological record. The capital is usually a large site, often with multiple mounds. Secondary centers usually contain fewer earthworks and may be smaller. According to one interpretation, the earthworks indicate an administrative function. From early historic accounts, we know that mounds often supported mortuary temples and the homes of the chiefs. Other towns farther down the hierarchy have no mounds and may be even smaller.

The term *paramount chiefdom* describes a chiefdom that has conquered or formed alliances with other chiefdoms, both simple and complex. A paramount chief is thus a chief of chiefs. Coosa was a paramount chiefdom by the time Hernando de Soto visited it in 1540. How Coosa attained this position of dominance is still far from certain.

Mississippian towns were often fortified when located on the boundary of a chiefdom or when especially important. Fortifications might take the form of palisade walls, sometimes with defensive towers and defensive ditches. Within the town was a political center with a townhouse or temple, or both. In the capital, this center included a chief's house. Such public buildings were often placed upon flat-topped, earthen mounds, usually of a pyramid shape (fig. 5). These mounds were constructed over long periods by occasional additions. Some mounds reached a height of sixty feet in Georgia, but smaller mounds were more common in northwest Georgia. The mounds served to elevate the elite above the commoners. They further served as a visual symbol of the power of the chief and

5. Mississippian platform mound. Photo by the author.

the center of the chiefdom. They also served as important symbols of a religious cult devoted to renewal rituals (Knight 1989). One of the public buildings usually served as a mortuary temple. Here the physical remains of the ancestors of the chief were buried or stored in baskets. Thus, a chief would only have to point to the mortuary temple and recite the family's genealogy to prove the legitimacy with which he or she ruled.

Next to these public buildings, and sometimes enclosing them, was a rectangular open courtyard or plaza. This area served as outdoor public space. It was a place to hold recreational games and often to torture enemy captives. Surrounding it were the homes of the residents. According to the de Soto reports, higher-ranking people lived near the chiefs on the edge of the plaza, and lower-ranking people lived nearer to the perimeter of the town (Varner and Varner 1951:171).

Natives in the area usually constructed two types of houses, winter houses and summer houses, paired in the village. Winter houses, usually square, were constructed of upright posts, either set into wall trenches (Early Mississippian) or individual postholes (Late Mississippian and historic periods). Small branches or pieces of cane were woven between the posts. This "fabric" was plastered with mud to form the walls of the house, a construction technique called "wattle and daub." The roof was cone shaped or pitched and consisted of a wooden superstructure covered with woven mats, canes, grass thatch, or sometimes even earth. Inside the house, the central area with its hearth was used for cooking and other domestic chores and the perimeter for storage and sleeping benches. By the late prehistoric period, it was common practice to construct the house in a pit excavated a foot or two deep. Dirt from the pit was banked against the walls outside, creating a well-insulated structure. These houses had narrow entrance tunnels through the embankments. Each dwelling housed one family. At the King site, house floor area averaged 60 square meters (Hally and Kelly 1998:52).

Summer houses were far simpler structures consisting of widely spaced wall posts and thatched roofs. They were usually rectangular and built at ground level, unlike the semi-subterranean winter houses. They were actually little more than sunshades. Summer houses are often difficult to define because of their flimsy nature and the maze of postholes archaeologists find at Mississippian sites, but we can sometimes locate them from the cluster of burials placed within them. Summer houses from the Early Mississippian period have not been identified in northwest Georgia, but it is likely that they are present. However, sixteenth-century summer houses have been identified at the Toqua site (Polhemus 1987) and sites of the Mouse Creek phase (Sullivan 1987) in eastern Tennessee. They have also been identified at the King (Hally and Kelly 1998) and Leake sites in northwest Georgia.

The Mississippian period saw the widespread acceptance of another innovation: shell-tempered pottery. Pottery that has been strengthened by adding crushed river-mussel shell to the clay is technologically superior to pottery tempered with sand, grit, fiber, or clay fragments (Steponaitis 1983). This form of pottery quickly spread throughout much of the Southeast, becoming common in eastern Tennessee and, to a lesser extent, northwest Georgia.

Some chiefs were treated as divine or semi-divine. They were entitled to a special diet, eating only the best cuts of meat and choicest vegetables. On certain occasions they were carried on litters borne on the shoulders of their people so their feet never touched the ground. They displayed symbols of their elite status, including large plates of beaten copper worn on the head, feather garments, and certain styles of marine-shell ornaments. They often carried other symbols of their power: fancy war axes and long flint swords. From later descriptions of the Natchez Indians of the Lower Mississippi Valley, we know that chiefs had other privileges. Commoners could never see them eating. They were greeted in special ways, and commoners could never stand above them. If the chief seated himself, commoners had to prostrate themselves. The treatment of the chief is reminiscent of that given to European monarchs in the Middle Ages.

The Mississippian Period in Northwest Georgia

The story of the Coosa people begins in the valley of the Coosawattee River. The ecotone between the Piedmont and the Ridge and Valley provinces in this area is known as the Cartersville Fault. The homeland of the Coosa people during the Mississippian period stretched from the point where the Coosawattee River crosses the fault to its junction with the Conasauga River, fourteen miles downstream.

Table 1 provides an overview of the Mississippian archaeology of northern Georgia. The first archaeological phase of the Mississippian period in the Coosa homeland is known as the Woodstock Culture (Cobb and Garrow 1996). Woodstock settlements are known from the Coosawattee Valley. The best-reported location is the Potts' Tract site (Hally 1970) (see fig. 6). Woodstock sites produce pottery types that can be seen as direct descendants of earlier Woodland period types. However, their identification as Mississippian hinges on changes in community organization in the form of fortified settlements. The Woodstock Fort (9Ck85), located in the Allatoona Reservoir, was a fortified village of many houses. A palisade with bastions and a ditch encircled the village. Evidence of mound building during the Woodstock period is scarce, but the Summerour Mound on the Chattahoochee River, excavated by Joseph Caldwell (1958:48), appears to have been a pyramid mound with a rectangular building on the summit (see Pluckhahn 1996 for a different interpretation). Although Woodstock is a poorly known culture, the evi-

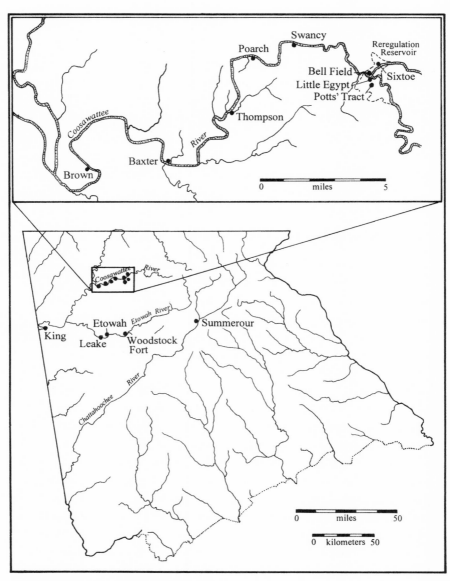

6. Mississippian sites. Map by Julie Barnes Smith.

Table 1. Mississippian archaeological phases of northwestern Georgia

Period	Date	Coosa drainage phase	Etowah drainage phase
Emergent	900	Woodstock	Woodstock
Mississippian	950	Woodstock	Woodstock
Early Mississippian	1000	Early Etowah	Early Etowah
	1050	Early Etowah	Early Etowah
	1100	Late Etowah	Late Etowah
	1150	Late Etowah	Late Etowah
Middle Mississippian	1200	Savannah	Unoccupied?
	1250		Early Wilbanks
	1300	Unnamed (Bell Field)	Early Wilbanks
	1325	Unnamed (Bell Field)	Late Wilbanks
Late Mississippian	1350	Little Egypt	Late Wilbanks
	1375	Little Egypt	Stamp Creek
	1400	Little Egypt	Stamp Creek
	1425	Little Egypt	Mayes
	1450	Little Egypt	Mayes
	1475	Barnett	Brewster
	1500	Barnett	Brewster
	1525	Barnett	Brewster
	1550	Barnett	Brewster
	1575	Barnett	

Sources: Hally and Langford 1988; King 1997.

dence of mound architecture and a centralized population living in a fortified town suggest the beginnings of the Mississippian lifestyle.

Within the Coosawattee Valley, five settlements with Woodstock occupations have been identified (Hally and Langford 1988:42). The population at these sites appears to have been small. No large Woodstock village site is known from this area. At the Potts' Tract site (9Mu103), a sheet midden (ground-level refuse aggregation) and several refuse-filled storage pits were excavated. Food remains in the pits included corn, acorn, walnut, hickory nut, and a variety of seeds. Other food remains included deer, bird, turtle, fish, and a variety of mollusks (Hally and Langford 1988:43). Evidence of houses was lacking in the area excavated. At this period of transition between Woodland and Mississippian lifeways, the Coosawattee Valley was not a major population center, nor was it the

location of any important political power. All this was to change in the
following period.

Following the Woodstock Culture in the Coosawattee Valley was the
Etowah Culture, a clear lineal descendant based on pottery designs. We
can divide Etowah into early and late subperiods (Hally and Langford
1988) based on changes in ceramic styles and a few radiocarbon dates.
During the early Etowah period, ca. A.D. 1000–1100, there is evidence of
increasing political complexity in the valley. The Sixtoe Field Mound site
(Kelly et al. 1965) was apparently constructed as the capital of an emerging chiefdom (see fig. 6). Unfortunately, evidence for other Etowah sites
in the valley is not plentiful. Two additional Etowah archaeological sites
are known, 9G05 and 9G09, but it is not known if they date to the early
or late Etowah period.

The Sixtoe Mound site consists of one flat-topped mound and a village
area of unknown size. Excavations by A. R. Kelly revealed two construction stages to the mound. A third stage of construction may once have
existed, its summit subsequently destroyed by historic plowing and erosion (Hally and Langford 1988:51). Kelly estimated that the original
height of the mound was 6 to 7 feet (ca. 2 m). He excavated only half of
the mound, but his work in that area of the summit revealed at least four
rectangular buildings, built one over the other. The largest building was
40 by 70 feet (12 by 20 m). The structures were of the wall-trench construction style. It is likely one or more buildings are on the southern half
of the mound that he did not excavate. Paired buildings on the mound
summit are known for the Hiwassee Island Mound in Tennessee, built at
roughly the same time (Hally and Langford 1988:52; Lewis and Kneberg
1946). There was some evidence that the mound faced northeast (judging
from a possible ramp on that side) and that it had a low terrace extension
on its western side.

In and around the mound summit building were twenty-three burials.
Both adults and children were present, suggesting that this was the ruling
kin group. Grave goods were scarce. One adult burial (sex indeterminate)
included a nine-inch broken stone bipointed ceremonial knife blade. This
was not a clear burial accompaniment, as the four pieces were scattered in
the grave pit fill. Two other burials contained shell beads. Although not
from a burial, one other artifact hints at the rich imagery that was part
of the emerging Mississippian ceremonial system—a stone earspool in-

scribed with a "weeping eye" motif, found during the initial clearing of
the mound. This earspool closely resembled one found by Joseph Caldwell at the Wilbanks site in the Allatoona Survey of the nearby Etowah
River Valley (Kelly et al. 1965:212). While these grave goods were not
spectacular, some effort was spent on grave preparation. Many of the
mound burials were partially enclosed or marked by slabs of limestone or
other stone. These were not true stone-box graves of the type found in
Tennessee and at the Etowah site. They were less formal but nonetheless
signaled special treatment of the dead.

Food remains from Sixtoe include deer, small animal, fish, turtle, fresh-
water mollusks, acorns, hickory nut, and corn. One basketry-lined pit
contained an abundance of charred corn.

Pottery from Sixtoe is decorated with complicated stamped patterns.
These patterns were carved on a wooden paddle and pressed into the clay
before firing. They were first identified at the Etowah site, an important
center located thirty-five miles to the south on the Etowah River (see chapter 4). Thus we arrive at the name "Etowah complicated stamped pottery." These same patterns are common from eastern Tennessee through
central Alabama and Georgia. The shared patterns probably do not
indicate any overall political unification but do show some cultural connections, probably through trade and intermarriage over a large area.

While Sixtoe pottery has patterns common over a large region, its
temper differs from that of sites from the same period in Tennessee and
more southerly areas of Georgia. Sixtoe pottery is tempered with limestone. Eastern Tennessee Hiwassee Island complicated stamped pottery is
tempered with shell. Etowah Valley pottery is tempered mostly with sand
or shell. Thus there are regional variants of the styles represented by the
Etowah patterns.

Kelly (Kelly et al. 1965:137–38) noted that the ceramics changed little
during the occupation of the mound. However, there was perhaps more
influence from the Etowah site near the end of the occupation. This
change may correspond to the rise of the Etowah site to regional promi-
nence. Based on analysis of collections from the village, Hally and Langford (1988) place Sixtoe Mound in the early Etowah period. Kelly placed
it in late Etowah, noting the presence of both Wilbanks ceramics and
painted or negative-painted shards on the mound. These suggest continued occupation of the site into the later Savannah period.

Excavations in the Sixtoe village area yielded evidence of wall-trench domestic structures of the Etowah Culture. While no complete house pattern was exposed, one nearly complete structure measured twenty feet long. The width was incomplete, but such houses were usually square. This house size is similar to more complete structures from later contexts, suggesting little change in family size. Village burials were found in refuse-filled storage pits and in burial pits.

We know little of this occupation of the Coosawattee Valley, but the presence of a site with a mound is thought to represent the administrative center of a chiefdom. Thus this site signals the beginnings of political complexity in the valley that was to result in the Coosa Paramount Chiefdom. There was an important center present in the area from this point until the valley was abandoned at the end of the sixteenth century.

Late Etowah occupation in the valley shifted downstream to another mound center, the Baxter site, 9Go8 (see fig. 6). There is some question whether Sixtoe Mound continued to be occupied. Although evidence is largely lacking, Hally and Langford (1988:55) suggest a possible continued occupation of the site, pointing to the destroyed upper layer(s) of the mound. They suggest that further analysis of collections could indicate whether there was a late occupation of Sixtoe. There is an unquestioned major occupation of the Baxter site in the late Etowah period. Apparently this site was the political center of the valley during the period ca. A.D. 1100–1200. Therefore, Baxter represents the founding of a new center. The site today (Hally and Langford 1988; Langford and Smith 1990) consists of a bulldozed mound remnant on the northern bank of the Coosawattee River. It measures two to three meters in height. It was formerly reported to have been six or seven meters high (19–23 ft), with a large surrounding village area of six hectares (14.8 acres). The site is centrally located within the part of the Coosawattee River west of the Cartersville fault—an ideal location for controlling the farmlands of the valley. Baxter is known only from surface collections and interviews with people who vandalized the site. It has been a favorite digging locale for untrained collectors for several years, and their activities have largely destroyed it. Little is known about this site, but its position as the dominant site in the valley during late Etowah is assured. Indeed, the Baxter Mound was the largest earthwork in the valley before its destruction. The village size of six hectares is also the largest in the valley. There are other Etowah settlements in the Coosawattee area, but they are poorly dated. It is suspected, however, that there are other late Etowah sites that paid allegiance to Baxter. The large size of the Baxter site probably is the result of population growth in the valley.

Power in the valley shifted to yet another new site during Middle Mississippian times, A.D. 1200–1350. This new location was the Bell Field Mound and village (9Mu101) (see fig. 6). Political authority in the area returned to a location near the ecotone and away from the center of the area. This was not far from the earlier Sixtoe site. In northern Georgia, this is the time of the Wilbanks cultural phase of the Savannah period. The Bell Field site has yielded only a small sample of pottery. Hally and Langford (1988:62) argue that this pottery does not appear to be typical of Wilbanks occupations on the Etowah River to the south. These southerly occupations are where the Wilbanks Culture was first defined. Hally and Langford suggest that the evidence may point out the need to define a new phase, but more data are needed to warrant such a step. For now it is enough to state that the Bell Field occupation occurred parallel to the Wilbanks phase occupations. In general, the Bell Field pottery appears more like the Dallas Culture pottery in eastern Tennessee and less similar to pottery found in the Etowah Valley of Georgia.

The size of the Bell Field village was not determined because alluvial soils from flooding had covered the site and because the excavators had concentrated on the mound during reservoir salvage. Farming or erosion had largely destroyed the Bell Field mound. It stood only two meters high when investigated by A. R. Kelly in the 1960s. Kelly recognized five to six stages of construction in the mound remnant. Informants stated that the mound had formerly been "at least six feet higher" (about 2 m) than at the time of his investigations (Kelly 1970:8). Kelly investigated two different superimposed mound summits (different stages of construction) and reported four tightly clustered rectangular buildings on each summit. These buildings were on different levels. The two buildings on the southwestern half of the mound were on a level one meter higher than the buildings on the other half. The buildings were of single post construction, with wall trench passageways connecting the buildings. Contrast this pattern of four buildings on the summit of Bell Field Mound with the earlier (probable) two buildings on the summit of the Sixtoe Mound, and we have a picture of evolving political complexity. It is likely that each building on the mound served a separate function, such as chief's home, mortuary temple, public meeting house, and the like. If so, the more buildings on a mound, or the more mounds in a site, the more political and religious functions the center served.

A series of log tombs was found intruding into one of the buildings on the summit of the Bell Field mound. These burials apparently originated in an upper stage of the mound that had been destroyed by farming and erosion. These tombs contained the remains of adult males buried with elaborate grave goods, probably symbolic of their chiefly status (fig. 7). Such material as finely crafted, negative-painted dog and human effigy pots probably made in Tennessee, copper headdress and earspools, a shell cup for the black drink ceremony (discussed in chap. 4), a large flint knife or sword, shell beads, and such exotic materials as a sawfish bill, are evidence of long-distance trade connections with many areas. It is clear that the Coosawattee Valley was not isolated at this time. Rather, it was part of an exchange network that connected elites throughout a large region.

B

7. Bell Field Mound artifacts. *A*, negative-painted dog effigy pot; *B*, human effigy bowl; *C*, flint "sword"; *D*, stone human effigy pipe, 142 mm long. Photos courtesy of Richard W. Jefferies.

C

D

At least one other site of this period is known from the Coosawattee Valley. The Poarch Farm site, 9Go1, has an area occupied at this time (see fig. 6). This site has not been excavated by professional archaeologists. However, evidence from testing, surface collecting, and comments by amateur diggers suggest that this settlement may have been a village. There is also some evidence seen in pottery styles that the Baxter site may still have been occupied (Langford and Smith 1990). However, this is not conclusive. It appears two sites were occupied at this time. Bell Field with its platform mound and elite burials evidently was the capital. The Poarch site was an allied village.

The main power center of this period, ca. A.D. 1200–1350, was the Etowah site, located about thirty-five miles to the south (see fig. 6), at the point where the Etowah River flows across the Cartersville Fault into the Ridge and Valley Province (Hally and Langford 1988; Larson 1989). At its height Etowah had six mounds. The village area covered twenty-one hectares (52 acres) and was surrounded by a fortification wall with towers and a large ditch 9 meters wide and 3 meters deep for added protection. Three large substructure mounds dominate the site. Mound A is 18 meters high, Mound B is 10.5 meters high, and Mound C is 7.5 meters high. A large plaza area, measuring 100 meters on a side and paved with clay 50 centimeters thick, lies adjacent to Mound A and Mound B. Three smaller mounds, now greatly reduced by plowing and erosion, lie to the east of the plaza. The Etowah site is preserved as a state park located just outside of Cartersville, Georgia.

Mound C has been excavated three times. John P. Rogan of the Smithsonian Institution first excavated the mound in the late nineteenth century, Warren K. Moorehead excavated it in the early twentieth century, and Lewis Larson conducted the final excavation in the mid-twentieth century. These excavations have revealed much of the splendor that was Etowah. Mound C was the location of the mortuary temple of the Etowah ruling elite. Their remains were interred within special tombs in the mound and surrounding its base. Larson (1971b) has argued there was hereditary rule at Etowah. He based his conclusion on the presence of this special burial area. (Commoners were buried in the village area.) He also points to the burials of infants and children that were accompanied by rich grave offerings. These offerings symbolized their elite status through inheritance rather than achievement of chiefly titles. The quantity, quality, and exotic nature of the symbols of power at Etowah are most impressive (see plate 1), and far surpass anything else found on this time level in the Ridge and Valley Province. That this power continued for several generations is supported by the richly accompanied burials associated with several stages of mound construction. The sheer size of the large mounds at Etowah offers further support. The village area at Etowah is many times the size of any other Mississippian site in northern Georgia. Its nearest rival for village size, and number and size of mounds, is the more spectacular Moundville Site, located 200 miles to the southwest in western Alabama.

Because of its large size, little is known about the growth and development of the Etowah site despite the many seasons of excavation that have taken place. It is known that Etowah was a large concern as early as the early Etowah period, A.D. 1000–1100. Etowah appears to have reached its peak as an important center during the Wilbanks phase of the Middle Mississippian period. Larson (1989) argues that all the elite burials in Mound C date to this one phase, perhaps within a few generations. There seems to have been a decline in the site after the Wilbanks occupation. Evidence for a continued occupation into the early Lamar period is missing. It appears that the site may have been abandoned from ca. 1350 to 1500, and then reoccupied during the sixteenth century. Spanish trade goods have been found in Lamar village burials. This Lamar occupation of the site was on the eastern side of the Wilbanks plaza. There is little evidence that the large mounds were used during Lamar times. Also, the Lamar village size is considerably smaller than the area occupied during the Wilbanks phase.

The political unit of which the Etowah site is surely the capital consists of eleven other sites. Four of these sites have one mound each, and at least seven sites without mounds are within ten miles downstream on the Etowah River (Hally and Langford 1988:65–66). It is clear that a multilevel political hierarchy was in operation in the Etowah Valley during this phase.

In its heyday, Etowah was certainly the dominant site in the Ridge and Valley Province. Distinctive status markers, such as embossed copper plates, styles of shell gorgets (Brain and Phillips 1996), and other luxury items of the types found at Etowah are also found north into Tennessee. The shared artistic tradition, apparently reflecting a belief in the same supernatural creatures depicted in the art, suggests a common cultural connection. On the other hand, Wilbanks pottery from the Etowah site represents an entirely different style tradition from that found in the Dallas Culture sites in the eastern Tennessee portion of the Ridge and Valley Province.

The Coosawattee Valley is intermediate between the Tennessee River sites and Etowah. It is notable that domestic and ceremonial ceramics here show characteristics from both areas. Thus, this area acted as a cultural bridge between the Dallas sites and Etowah. It is likely there were connections between the elites of Etowah, the Coosawattee chiefdom at Bell Field, and sites in eastern Tennessee. We can only speculate about what these connections were. Perhaps they constituted political dominance by Etowah in a paramount chiefdom. Perhaps they were loose alliances based on payment of tribute to Etowah. Maybe they were less binding exchanges of prestige goods and perhaps marriage partners between elites. There may have been some other connection. The important factor to note is that shortly after Etowah lost its power around A.D. 1350–1375, the Coosawattee chiefdom began its ascent to power.

Following the occupation at the Bell Field Mound, the center of power in the valley again shifted. However, this time the shift was only a short distance across the Coosawattee River to the Little Egypt archaeological site (see fig. 6). The continual shifting of the seat of power in the Coosawattee Valley is noteworthy. In many areas of the Southeast, chiefdoms appear to be stable through time. For example, many mound sites grew for centuries, until the mounds became quite large. The Etowah site is a possible example. Assuming that Mound A was begun when the site was founded in early Etowah times, the mound grew to a height of 18 meters during the 350 years after ca. A.D. 1000. By contrast, the Coosawattee Valley had three sequential mound centers during this time, and a fourth immediately after it.

How can we interpret this phenomenon? Chiefdoms in general are ruled by a high-ranking family group, or lineage, who legitimize their power by claiming direct descent from founding (often mythological) ancestors. This right to rule is often expressed in ancestor worship. The remains of the revered ancestors are stored in a mortuary temple, such as Mound C at Etowah or the log tombs in the Bell Field Mound. The chief uses this direct link with ancestral rulers to confirm his right to rule.

Because of this desire to display connections with founding ancestors, there is a tendency to remain in one place for long periods. The situation in the Coosawattee Valley suggests that local chiefdoms were not stable, but were constantly being overthrown. The new ruler would have no reason to suggest that his ancestors had ruled the valley for generations. The chief, whether male or female (Hernando de Soto's chroniclers report male and female chiefs in the sixteenth century), symbolized the founding of a new regime by changing the location of the capital. Chiefdoms often tend to be cyclical, having periods of rise and fall (Anderson 1990, 1994; DePratter 1983), and the Coosawattee Valley appears to contain clear evidence of factions competing for power. Lewis Larson (1972) explored the role of warfare in southeastern chiefdoms, so conquest cannot be ruled out. Whatever the reasons, we know there were four centers of power in the Coosawattee Valley during the Mississippian period. These changes in the location of the capital suggest there were at least four shifts in the ruling lineage.

The Little Egypt site (Hally 1979, 1980) consists of two or perhaps three mounds arranged around a plaza area with a surrounding village measuring approximately five hectares. Although badly damaged by plowing, erosion, and early excavation, the two largest mounds were more than 2.5 meters high. Warren K. Moorehead mentioned a third mound when he visited the site early in this century. However, David Hally of the University of Georgia found no evidence of it when he conducted major excavations in the 1970s.

The Little Egypt site was founded during a period archaeologists call the Little Egypt phase, A.D. 1350–1475. During this phase, at least four construction stages were completed on Mound A and a sizable village grew up. During the following Barnett phase, A.D. 1475–1575, the village continued to grow and the second (and perhaps a third) mound was constructed.

Excavations during the 1970s concentrated on the village area. Extensive trenching located several domestic structures. Eventually three structures in the village and two on Mound A were excavated. Work on Mound A also yielded several burials. None of these burials were as elaborate as the log tomb burials from the earlier Bell Field Mound or Etowah Mound C. Nonetheless, they were accompanied by pottery vessels, shell ornaments, and other items. Burials excavated by Warren K.

Moorehead contained a large stone knife, shell gorgets, a stone axe, and portions of a sixteenth-century European sword. However, in general, sixteenth-century Lamar Culture burials are not accompanied by the wealth of exotic materials that characterized earlier, Middle Mississippian burials found at Bell Field or Etowah.

The Little Egypt site was not the only site occupied during the Late Mississippian period in the Coosawattee Valley. During the Little Egypt phase, the Baxter site may have been occupied, while the Thompson site was established between Baxter and Little Egypt. The Thompson site is little known, but has one small mound and a village size of 2.43 hectares (ha). It thus appears there were perhaps three towns or villages in the valley at this time, perhaps signaling an increase in population. We may assume the mound at Thompson served an administrative function and therefore the Thompson site was a secondary administrative center. Based on this, we may conclude that this period saw the appearance of a complex chiefdom in the valley—that is, a chiefdom with at least three levels of settlement.

By the Barnett phase, which dates to the sixteenth century, there is good evidence of population expansion in the Coosawattee Valley. At least six villages and two smaller settlements are known from this period. The Little Egypt site, with its two or three mounds and 5-hectare village, seems to be the capital. The Thompson site, located downstream midway in the concentration of villages, measures 2.4 ha, has one mound, and is considered a secondary administrative center during this phase. The Baxter site had a late Lamar village of about 2 ha and the Poarch Farm site has a village of 3.3 ha. New villages were established at the Swancy site (1.76 ha) and the Brown Farm site (5.5 ha). There is also evidence of occupation of the Potts' Tract site. Here Hally (1970) excavated three houses; however, he was unable to determine the size of the site. It was owned by more than one landowner, and Hally was able to get permission to work in only one portion. Potts' Tract is believed to be a hamlet (that is, a settlement of two or three families), although it may represent a small village (a settlement larger than a hamlet).

There is also evidence for the occupation of a village area around the Sixtoe Mound that dates to this time. Kelly and his associates (1965) recovered a European metal "dirk" or dagger from a burial here, but the size of the occupation is not known. A small farmstead has been located on the Oostanaula River just downstream from the mouth of the Coosa-wattee.

Hally, Smith, and Langford estimate a population of the valley at 2,500 to 4,650 people in the sixteenth century (1990:126). This estimate is based on (1) the number of sites, (2) their area, (3) an estimate of people per area of an average site (based on more complete excavations at the King site described below), and (4) formulas for determining population from house area.

This description encapsulates what is known about the late prehistoric settlement of the Coosawattee Valley through archaeology. We now turn our attention to the records of the sixteenth-century Spanish explorers who entered the region.

3

Spanish Exploration

The First Light of History

Three major Spanish expeditions entered Coosa during the sixteenth century. Each expedition gives us some information on the chiefdom.

Hernando de Soto, 1540

Hernando de Soto sought a civilization to conquer. He had been a major lieutenant in Pizarro's conquest of Peru and was a fabulously wealthy man. Yet he longed for a territory of his own. He was sufficiently prosperous to be able to loan money to the king of Spain, so apparently fame, not wealth, was his goal. Alas, there was no high civilization in eastern North America, and de Soto died a broken man on the banks of the Mississippi River.

With the Hernando de Soto expedition, the Coosa region enters the historic period (fig. 8). There are three chronicles of the expedition written by participants: the account of Rodrigo Ranjel (1904; Clayton, Knight, and Moore 1993), de Soto's secretary; the account of an anonymous Portuguese Gentleman of Elvas; and the short account of the king's factor on the expedition, Luys Biedma (Clayton, Knight, and Moore 1993; Smith

1968). There is also a history of the expedition written by a Peruvian, Garcilaso de la Vega (Clayton, Knight, and Moore 1993; Varner and Varner 1951), who interviewed members of the expedition many years after the fact. His account is considered to be the least reliable, as it conflicts in many instances with the other three relations, but it does offer information not available elsewhere.

When de Soto arrived in the Ridge and Valley Province in northeastern Tennessee in 1540, he immediately heard of Coosa. Indeed, he had first become aware of Coosa months earlier when he was in the Province of Ocute on the Oconee River in Piedmont eastern Georgia (see fig. 8). Upon entering the Ridge and Valley after crossing the Appalachian Mountains, de Soto visited the chiefdom of Chiaha, a fortified town believed to have been located on Zimmerman's Island in the French Broad River (Hudson et al. 1985). He was told by the Indians that Chiaha was subject to a chief of Coca (Coosa) (Clayton, Knight, and Moore 1993 1:85; Elvas 1968: 65). De Soto's army rested at Chiaha for thirty days.

As he continued traveling in a southerly direction down the Ridge and Valley, de Soto came into contact with other Indian groups who were allied with Coosa (DePratter, Hudson, and Smith 1985; Hudson 1990a, 1997). Many of their villages are unnamed. After seven days' travel, they reached the territory of the chief of Coste. The main town of Coste is believed to have been on Bussell Island at the junction of the Tennessee and Little Tennessee rivers. The army stayed in Coste for several days and then traveled for part of a day to the town of Tali, which was probably located up the Little Tennessee River at either the Toqua or Tomotley archaeological site (Hudson 1990a). From here the army traveled south, perhaps along the Tellico River, following the edge of the Ridge and Valley along the ecotone with the Blue Ridge (that is, the Great Indian Warpath of the eighteenth century).

After leaving Tali, the Gentleman of Elvas states that "they traveled six days passing by many towns subject to the Cacique [chief] of Coca [Coosa]" (Elvas 1968:75). Other sources reveal that one of these towns was called Tasqui (Ranjel 1904:111). For the next two days they passed several small villages. On the second day they came to the central town of the province of Coosa, believed to have been located at the Little Egypt archaeological site. (See discussion in chapter 5.) The chief of Coosa came out to greet de Soto: "This chief was a powerful one and a ruler of a wide

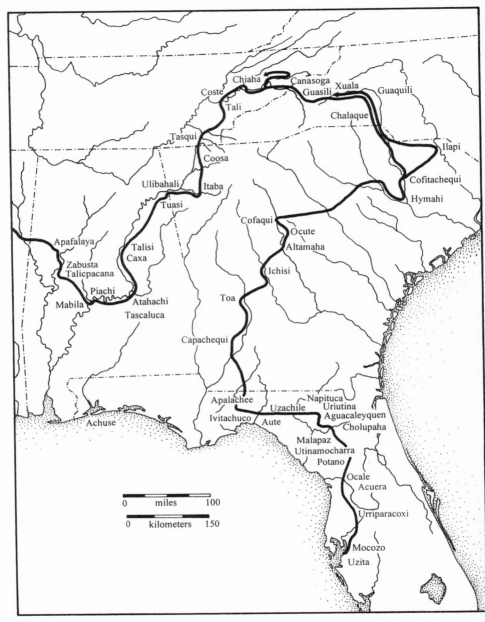

Chiaha Canasoga
Coste   Guasili Xuala Guaquili
        Tali
                    Chalaque
Tasqui
        Coosa   Ilapi
Ulibahali Itaba   Cofitachequi
    Tuasi   Hymahi
                    Cofaqui
Apafalaya   Ocute
    Zabusta   Talisi   Altamaha
    Talicpacana Caxa
        Piachi   Ichisi
Mabila   Atahachi
            Tascaluca   Toa

                    Capachequi

        Apalachee   Napituca
                Uzachile Uriutina
        Ivitachuco   Aute Aguacaleyquen
Achuse   Cholupaha
                    Malapaz
                    Utinamocharra
                        Potano
                            Ocale
                            Acuera

        0   miles   100
                            Urriparacoxi
        0   kilometers 150

                            Mocozo
                            Uzita

8. The explorations of Hernando de Soto. Map by Julie Barnes Smith.

territory, one of the best and most abundant that they found in Florida. And the chief came out to receive the Governor in a litter covered with the white mantles of the country, and the litter was borne on the shoulders of sixty or seventy of his principal subjects, with no plebeian or common Indian among them; and those that bore him took turns by relays with great ceremonies after their manner" (Ranjel 1904:112).

The Gentleman of Elvas continues, "The Cacique came out to receive him at the distance of two crossbow-shot from the town, borne in a litter on the shoulders of his principal men, seated on a cushion, and covered with a mantle of marten-skins, of the size and shape of a woman's shawl: on his head he wore a diadem of plumes, and he was surrounded by many attendants playing upon flutes and singing" (Elvas 1968:75–76).

Coosa was a rich land. The granaries contained much stored corn and beans, and mention is made of plums, wild "apples," and wild grapes. "The country, thickly settled in numerous and large towns, with fields between, extending from one to another, was pleasant, and had a rich soil with fair river margins" (Elvas 1968:76).

De Soto took the Coosa chief hostage and chained up many of his people to serve as burden bearers for his expedition. The army rested in Coosa for twenty-five days but eventually set out to discover new lands. De Soto forced the chief of Coosa to go with him. The first day he passed through the town of Tallimuchase (near present-day Fairmount, Georgia) and the next day came to the town of Ytaua, said to be subject to Coosa (Elvas 1968:78). Ytaua (also spelled Itaba), probably the Etowah archaeological site, was by 1540 little more than a minor Lamar-period village (DePratter, Hudson, and Smith 1985; Hudson 1990a, 1997). Here floodwaters forced de Soto to wait for six days, but he finally crossed the Etowah River and set out toward Ulibahali, located downstream and to the west. While at Ytaua, the Spanish "bought" some Indian women in exchange for mirrors and knives (Ranjel 1904:113).

Ulibahali was described as a fortified town, with a second town located across the river. The chief of Ulibahali met de Soto with a show of force in an attempt to free the chief of Coosa because they were his subjects (Ranjel 1904:113). The chief of Coosa stepped in and stopped the impending battle, restoring peaceful relations. Ulibahali furnished additional carriers to de Soto, and the expedition moved on. The wild grapes of Ulibahali were said to be the best the Spaniards ate. Ulibahali is believed to have been located near present Rome, Georgia, at the headwaters of the Coosa River.

The expedition left Ulibahali and spent the next night at a small village near the river. The day after, they went to Piachi and a day or two later reached the town of Tuasi. After passing through additional villages for several days, they came to the town of Talisi, located near a fine river. Talisi is believed to be near present-day Childersburg, Alabama. By the time de Soto arrived, the town had been abandoned. Eventually the chief of Talisi returned and agreed to give burden bearers to de Soto. At this point de Soto released the chief of Coosa, allowing him to return to his home, but he kept Coosa's sister. At Talisi, an emissary from the next paramount chief, Tascaluca, visited de Soto. Evidence from the later expedition of Tristán de Luna suggests that Talisi was the last town subject to Coosa.

Tristán de Luna, 1560

Twenty years after de Soto was there, a detachment of the Tristán de Luna expedition returned to the territory of Coosa (Hudson et al. 1989; Priestly 1928) (fig. 9). Following de Soto's failure to find exploitable wealth, Tristán de Luna returned to the Southeast in a colonizing venture. He brought Mexican Indians and Spaniards completely equipped to establish a permanent colony. The expedition was one of the largest and best supplied of any effort in the New World. The colonists landed in Pensacola Bay to begin their new lives, but, unfortunately, before they could unload the ships, a hurricane struck. The storm destroyed most of the ships and much of the cargo. With food supplies lost, Luna was forced to seek Indians in order to obtain food. The starving colonists moved into the interior of Alabama, reaching the Indian town of Nanipacana, which was probably on the Alabama River in modern Wilcox County.

Their situation continued to deteriorate, and Luna sent out a detachment of men under the command of Mateo del Sauz. They were to search for the rich province of Coosa, still remembered from the de Soto expedition. This group included about forty cavalry, a hundred infantry, and two friars. Some of Luna's soldiers were veterans of the de Soto expedition and remembered Coosa. They traveled very slowly because they lacked Indian guides and they were starving. After nearly a month, they

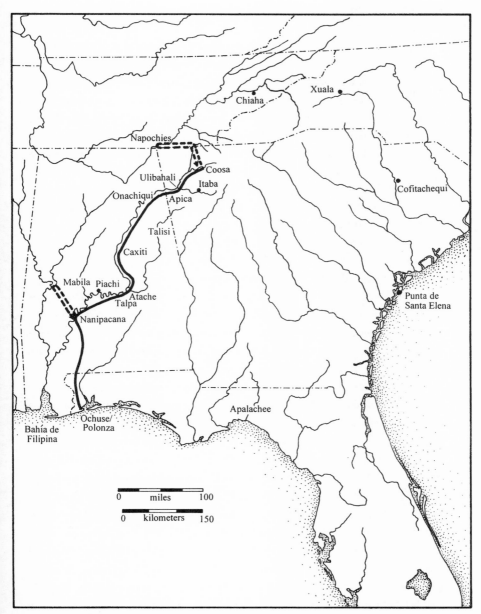

9. The route of Tristán de Luna. Map by Julie Barnes Smith.

reached the province of Taxcaluca (Tascaluca) near present-day Montgomery, Alabama.

Continuing toward the north, they reached the town of Caxiti. Although the Indian occupants had run away, the Spaniards found some hidden corn and shipped it downstream to Nanipacana. Then they continued toward Coosa. There is hardly any mention of Talisi, although a soldier, Alonso de Montalván, interviewed a year later, said that "Talis" was the first town of Coosa. Did he go to Talisi, or was he a veteran of the de Soto expedition who had been there before? The best available compilation of the survivors of the de Soto expedition does not mention Montalván (Avellaneda 1990), but the list is not complete and we cannot therefore assume that Montalván was not with de Soto. Perhaps the Sauz detachment did visit Talisi.

Sixteenth-century artifacts, which may have come from the Luna expedition, have been found at the Hightower archaeological site, near present-day Childersburg, Alabama. Specifically, an iron sickle blade was recovered (fig. 10). It is not likely that de Soto would have carried this artifact type, but the Luna expedition of colonists may have. Another sickle blade has been recovered from the Pine Log Creek site near present-day Mobile, Alabama (Stowe 1982). This is the area from which Luna's forces were later to depart.

Ten days from Caxiti, the Spaniards reached Onachiqui, also said to be the first town of Coosa by members of the expedition. The location of Onachiqui is unknown, but it may have been at or near the Polecat Ford site (1Ce308), where many Spanish artifacts have been found (Little and Curren 1981). Given the distances traveled and remaining to other Coosa towns, Onachiqui was probably near the town of Tuasi mentioned by de Soto's chroniclers (Hudson et al. 1989:40).

Continuing toward Coosa, the expedition reached the town of Apica, said to have been five or six leagues (approximately 13–20 miles) from Ulibahali. Apica must be one of the known protohistoric archaeological sites located downstream from present-day Rome, Georgia. The King site, Johnstone Farm site, Mohman site, and site 9Fl175 are all possible candidates for Apica. All appear to have been occupied at the correct time based on archaeological evidence. Both King and Johnstone Farm have produced sixteenth-century European artifacts; site 9Fl175 has never been excavated by professional archaeologists. Although the Luna narra-

0   5
CENTIMETERS

10. Sickle blade and other artifacts, Hightower Village site. Photos courtesy of Robert C. Wilson.

tives barely mentioned Apica, it is noteworthy since it seems to be the
same name as Abihka. Abihka was one of the leading towns of the Upper
Creeks in the eighteenth century. Certainly, it was an old town by the
eighteenth century, although its location changed, as we shall see.

From Apica, the expedition continued to Ulibahali, again believed to
be near the head of the Coosa River at present-day Rome, Georgia. There
are two archaeological sites in this area that could represent Ulibahali
(and remember that the de Soto narratives mention two towns on opposite sides of the river). There was a mound site located in the confluence
of the Etowah and Oostanaula Rivers, where the Coosa River forms.
Although this site has been destroyed by the construction of modern
Rome, Georgia, it was reported by C. C. Jones in the nineteenth century.
Jones claims that gold beads were recovered from this mound (Jones
1861:82–83), and, if true, they were probably of European manufacture
since the Indians did not use gold. There is a large, protohistoric village
site located a few hundred yards downstream, on the south bank of the
Coosa River (that is, across the water from Jones's mound). The construction of tennis courts and parking lots for the Coosa Country Club has
destroyed most of this site. However, salvaged pottery collections indicate that it was occupied around the de Soto dateline. The Luna forces
remained at Ulibahali for several days before continuing to Coosa.

Since the Luna narrators do not mention Itaba and Talimachusy, it is
likely that the Sauz detachment followed the Oostanaula River upstream
to Coosa instead of the Etowah River route taken by de Soto (Hudson et
al. 1989:40). By this route, Sauz and his men would have encountered all
the villages along the Coosawattee River leading up to the capital. The
province of Coosa was said to consist of eight towns in an area about two
leagues long (approximately 11.1 km). The Spaniards, some of whom
had been to Coosa with de Soto's forces, expected a rich province full of
food. What they found left them disillusioned. The account of Davila
Padilla is most informative:

> It was God's will that they should soon get within sight of that place
> which had been so far famed and so much thought about [Coosa]
> and, yet, it did not have above thirty houses, or a few more. There
> were seven little hamlets in its district, five of them smaller and two
> larger that Coza itself, which name prevailed for the fame it had
> enjoyed in its antiquity. It looked so much the worse to the Spaniards

for having been depicted so grandly, and they had thought it to be so much better. Its inhabitants had been said to be innumerable, the site itself as being wider and more level than Mexico, the springs had been said to be many and of very clear water, food plentiful and gold and silver in abundance, which, without judging rashly, was that which the Spaniards desired most. Truly the land was fertile, but it lacked cultivation. There was much forest, but little fruit, because as it was not cultivated the land was all unimproved and full of thistles and weeds. Those they had brought along as guides, being people who had been there before, declared that they must have been bewitched when this country seemed to them so rich and populated as they had stated. The arrival of the Spaniards in former years had driven the Indians up into the forests, where they preferred to live among the wild beasts who did no harm to them, but whom they could master, than among the Spaniards at whose hands they received injuries, although they were good to them. Those from Coza received the guests well, liberally, and with kindness, and the Spaniards appreciated this, the more so as the actions of their predecessors did not call for it. . . . Every day little groups of them went searching through the country and they found it all deserted and without news of gold. . . . The Spaniards have the fame of not being very humble and the people of Coza who had surrendered themselves experienced now their favors. Not only were they careful not to cause them any damage or injury, but gave them many things they had brought along, outside of what they gave in the regular exchange for maize. (Swanton 1922:231)

Domingo de la Anunciación, a friar on the expedition, gives a few more details: "This province of Coosa is somewhat better as regards the land and the forest, and much more densely populated than any we have left behind. There is a mountain range to the north of the town, which runs east and west. It is fairly high and well-wooded, but up to this time we do not know where it begins or ends. This town is situated on the banks of two small rivers which unite within it. Around the town there are some good savannahs, and a valley well peopled with Indians where they plant all they raise to eat. After one leaves here all the rest is forest" (Priestly 1928:241).

From these accounts, we learn many details of Coosa following the expedition of Hernando de Soto. Coosa was clearly on the decline. The villages were smaller than the de Soto veterans remembered, and accounts specifically mention a smaller population. The lack of lands in cultivation and the description of "thistles and weeds" evoke a picture of abandoned and overgrown old fields. Contrast this scene with that painted by the Gentleman of Elvas twenty years earlier, when Coosa was "thickly settled in numerous and large towns, with fields between, extending from one to another" (Elvas 1968:76).

Davila Padilla specifically mentions that two of the villages were larger than the capital of Coosa. Archaeologically, the Brown Farm site is larger than the Little Egypt site, the suggested capital with three mounds. It is not hard to imagine that the site size of another of the villages may have surpassed Coosa in 1560.

Trade is also evident in Coosa. The abundance of sixteenth-century European artifacts from the Coosawattee Valley bears out the passage of both the de Soto and Luna parties. Both amateur and professional excavations have recovered fragments of swords, metal chisel blades, a crossbow bolt tip, possible chain mail, glass beads, and brass bells of the period (see plate 2) (Langford and Smith 1990; Smith 1987, 1992:100). However, the most dramatic artifact recovered to date is a metal plate of brass or copper from the Poarch Farm site (Langford 1990). It was apparently manufactured in Mexico and engraved with Christian religious symbols in an Aztec native style (plate 2a; fig. 11). Since de Soto never traveled to Mexico, it is likely this artifact found its way to the Coosawattee Valley via the Sauz detachment of the Luna expedition (Langford 1990). No other area of the interior Southeast can boast such an extensive array of sixteenth-century Spanish goods.

The Indians fed Luna's men, and the detachment remained at Coosa for several months. In addition to trading for food, the Spaniards offered to accompany the Coosa Indians on a punitive raid (Hudson 1988; Swanton 1922). A former tributary, the Napochies, not only were refusing to pay tribute to Coosa but also were fighting with their former overlords. An expedition was organized to subjugate the Napochies. According to Davila Padilla, "The Indians set forward, and it was beautiful to see them divided up in eight different groups, two of which marched together in the four directions of the earth (north, south, east, and west)" (Swanton 1922:233). The Spaniards sent two detachments of troops, one of infantry and the other of cavalry. They marched two days to the Na-

11. Poarch Farm copper plate. Drawing by Julie Barnes Smith.

pochie villages, located on the Tennessee River near present-day Chattanooga, Tennessee (Hudson et al. 1989). The effort quickly subjugated the
Napochies, and the Spaniards returned to Coosa.

Shortly after this expedition, the Spaniards left Coosa to find the rest
of their forces. Luna's colony soon collapsed, and the survivors returned
to Mexico.

The Juan Pardo Expeditions

We next hear of Coosa from the expeditions of Juan Pardo in 1566–1568
(Beck 1997; DePratter, Hudson, and Smith 1983; Hudson 1990b) (fig.
12). Following permanent European settlement of the Atlantic coast
by Spaniards at St. Augustine and Santa Elena, interest in the interior
was renewed. The fledgling colony at Santa Elena, South Carolina, on
present-day Parris Island, was in bad condition, being short of food. Juan
Pardo was sent on an expedition, supposedly to find a road to the silver
mines in Zacatecas, Mexico, but more likely Pardo's detachment was sent
into the interior to live off the Indians. By this time the Spaniards realized
that they must attract a core of native allies for their colonizing venture to
succeed. Thus Pardo was also to pacify the Indians. He was loaded down

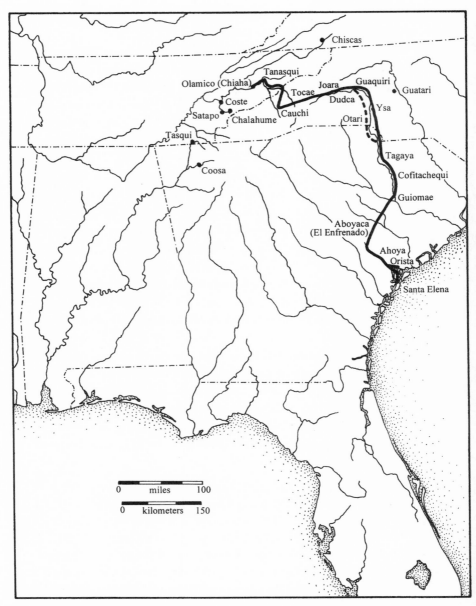

Chiscas

Tanasqui

Olamico (Chiaha)   Joara   Guaquiri
Tocae   Guatari
Coste   Dudca
                                 Ysa
Satapo   Cauchi
Chalahume   Otari

Tasqui   Tagaya

Coosa   Cofitachequi

                                 Guiomae

                      Aboyaca
                      (El Enfrenado)

                           Ahoya
                           Orista

                                 Santa Elena

0   miles   100
0   kilometers   150

12. The route of Juan Pardo. Map by Julie Barnes Smith.

with goods for trade and gift giving (DePratter and Smith 1980) and had been instructed not to antagonize the Indians.

The Pardo expedition set out on foot from Santa Elena. They traveled north across the coastal plain to Cofitachequi, the important center previously visited by de Soto. From this point they followed the route of de Soto. They traveled northward into present-day North Carolina and westward in the Great Valley of the Ridge and Valley Province in modern Tennessee. They visited Chiaha of de Soto expedition fame, and continued to the southwest to the Little Tennessee River Valley. From Chiaha on, they were in territory that was under the rule of Coosa in de Soto's day. When they reached the town of Satapo (probably the Citico archaeological site on the Little Tennessee River), they learned of an Indian plot against them. The chief of Coosa had organized the natives, including Uchi, Casque, and Olameco (Chiaha). They refused to give Pardo any food unless he paid for it, and they threatened to attack the Spaniards. Pardo was warned of three planned ambushes. The chief of Satapo refused to give him any burden bearers to continue southward toward Coosa. Rather than provoke bloodshed, Pardo decided to return to Santa Elena.

Although Pardo never reached the central towns of Coosa, some information is recorded in the narratives of the expedition. Coosa clearly still had influence over native groups in eastern Tennessee, at least as far as Chiaha. The nature of this alliance is not known; it might not have been as formal as in had been in the past. Juan de la Vandera, the notary of the Pardo expedition, recorded information from one soldier who traveled with Indians for five or six days to visit Coosa:

> The land is very lightly inhabited because there are no more than three small settlements. The first is two days' journey from Satapo and is called Tasqui. During these two days' journey there is good land and three large rivers. A bit further on [is] another place that is called Tasquiqui. A day's journey further [is] a destroyed town that is called Olitifar. All [the ground covered during this part of the journey] is good, flat land. From there two days' journey further on through uninhabited lands is a small settlement and beyond that, about a league, [is] Cosa. It is a large town, the largest there is [in the area] where we went from Santa Elena until you arrive at it. It must have about 150 householders, judging from the size of the town. It is

a place richer than any of those noted. Ordinarily there is a large number of Indians in it. It is situated in a low land in the lap of a mountain range. Around it at a half and a quarter of a league and at a league are many large settlements. It is a very abundant land. Its site is at the midday sun or less than at the midday sun. (Hudson 1990b:303)

This glimpse of the Tennessee Valley and upper Coosa drainage suggests that Coosa may have regained some of its power. There is no hint in the Pardo documents that Coosa had moved from the position it occupied in northwest Georgia in 1540. Indeed, the description of being situated in the lap of a mountain range perfectly fits the location of the Little Egypt site. Furthermore, Coosa apparently still had allies far into Tennessee along the edge of the Ridge and Valley Province.

Linguistic Affiliations of the Coosa Paramount Chiefdom

Only a few clues survive to indicate what languages the natives of sixteenth-century Coosa spoke, but these clues are important in efforts to link these people with groups known from later historic accounts. Evidence from language can be used to show population movements.

The linguistic affiliations of the Coosa people have been researched by Karen Booker and Robert Rankin in conjunction with Charles Hudson's research into the Juan Pardo expeditions (Booker, Hudson, and Rankin 1992; Hudson 1990b). Only a few words of the native language were recorded; the most common evidence is that of place-names.

Based on its name, the first town of Coosa visited by Pardo, Tanasqui, could be either Muskogean (a language family that includes languages of the Creek, Chickasaw, and Choctaw) or Cherokee. Chiaha, and its alternate name, Olamico, is believed to have been a Koasati-language place name. Koasati is another member of the Muskogean language family. On the Little Tennessee River, Chalahume and Satapo appear to be Muskogean words. The Pardo accounts mention the Casqui, and this name also seems to be Koasati. Hudson (1990b:106) suggests a link with the Caskinampo of the late seventeenth century on the Tennessee River. The Pardo accounts also mention the Yuchi. The Yuchi were an isolated language group not related to Muskogean or Cherokee and were apparently located somewhere in eastern Tennessee in the sixteenth century. Later they settled with the Lower Creeks on the Chattahoochee River and on the Savannah River. De Soto's Coste are also believed to have been Koasati speakers. Farther south, perhaps on the upper reaches of the Hiwassee River, the Tasquiqui probably spoke a dialect of Koasati. The Napochies probably spoke some dialect of Western Muskogean, that is, Choctaw or Chickasaw. The Coosa and Apica of the sixteenth century were probably Eastern Muskogean Creek speakers, while most of the people of eastern Tennessee were speakers of Koasati and related Muskogean dialects. It is of interest that the Cherokee, who populated eastern Tennessee and northwest Georgia in the eighteenth century, were newcomers to the area. The early Spanish accounts leave little doubt that the people of the paramount chiefdom of Coosa were all speakers of the Muskogean language family.

After 1568, Coosa again slips away from the reach of history because of a lack of written records. Spaniards ceased to travel to Coosa. What became of Coosa until Europeans again recorded its history in the late seventeenth century remains an archaeological problem. In the next chapter, we will examine the culture of Coosa and the Upper Creeks in the eighteenth century. Then we will return to the archaeology of sixteenth-century Coosa in chapter 5. Chapter 6 will use archaeological information to fill the void and link Coosa of the sixteenth century with that of the eighteenth century.

4

Coosa in the
Eighteenth Century

Following the Spanish entradas of the sixteenth century, no European set foot in Coosa country until sometime near the end of the seventeenth century. However, meaningful historical accounts did not appear until well into the eighteenth century. The towns of Coosa and Abihka, mentioned by the Spanish explorers, were important places in the eighteenth century. Therefore, anthropologists initially assumed that the well-known eighteenth-century locations of these towns were the same as in de Soto's day (Swanton 1939). Archaeological research in the late 1940s demonstrated that the eighteenth-century site of Coosa was not occupied in the sixteenth century (DeJarnette and Hansen 1960). Where, then, was Coosa during the sixteenth and seventeenth centuries? Before answering that question, this chapter will sketch what was known about Coosa of the eighteenth century.

Little was written about the Coosa-Abihka people during the eighteenth century. We know that Coosa and Abihka were important towns of the Upper Creeks, an amalgam of towns in three locations. The Coosa and Abihka towns were located on the Coosa River and its tributaries. The Okfuskee cluster of towns was located on the upper Tallapoosa River and the Tallapoosa cluster on the lower Tallapoosa River. Much of what we know about the Upper Creeks comes from descriptions of the Talla-poosas. The Tallapoosas in all probability had lived on the lower Tal-lapoosa River along the fall-line area since the sixteenth century, if not from even earlier times. Like their neighbors to the north on the Coosa, they began to accept refugees from many areas. By the eighteenth century they had become a mixed people.

By necessity, the following ethnographic sketch is based primarily on descriptions for the Tallapoosas, or Upper Creeks in general. We know that James Adair visited some of the Abihka towns, so his descriptions may be the most suitable for our purposes. It is not known how the culture of the Coosa-Abihka people differed from that of the Tallapoosas, if at all. The fact that they cooperated as Upper Creeks suggests that their cultures were close, but their archaeological remains show consistent, albeit minor, differences in such matters as pottery styles.

The Coosa-Abihka people were undergoing rapid culture changes throughout the time we are investigating. For this reason, I have chosen the period 1760–1775 as the basis of this characterization of Upper Creek culture. During this period, many Europeans visited the Upper Creeks, including William Bartram, James Adair, Jean-Bernard Bossu, Bernard Romans, and David Taitt. Little information exists about Creek social organization until the nineteenth and early twentieth centuries, so we must obtain this material from later sources.

Public Architecture and Housing

William Bartram visited the Upper Creeks in the 1770s (Waselkov and Braund 1995). He describes a typical town (probably one of the towns on the Tallapoosa River) as consisting of a rotunda, public square, and a "chunky-yard" (fig. 13). The rotunda was an enclosed circular structure used for council meetings and for housing visitors. It was a substantial structure, well insulated against the cold. William Bartram described the council house at Atasi, one of the Upper Creek Tallapoosa towns:

> The great council house, or rotunda is appropriated to much the same purpose as the public square, but more private, and seems particularly dedicated to political affairs; women and youth are never admitted; and I suppose, it is death for a female to presume to enter the door, or approach within its pale. It is a vast conical build-

ing or circular dome, capable of accommodating many hundred people; constructed and furnished within, exactly in the same manner as those of the Cherokees already described, but much larger than any I had seen of them: there are people appointed to take care of it, to have it daily swept clean, and to provide canes for fuel, or to give light. (Bartram 1928:357)

In the warmer months, the council met in the public square, also called the square ground or summer council house. The square ground consisted of four open sheds or arborlike buildings arranged around an open courtyard. In the center of the square, the sacred fire was maintained.

The chunky-yard consisted of a rectangular swept and weeded open area, often quite large. Bartram (1853:35) notes that some were three hundred yards long. In this open plaza the Creeks played the game of chunky. They also used it as a place for torturing war captives and conducting other social business.

Chunky was a favorite pastime of the Creeks and many other southeastern tribes. In this game for two players, one rolled a stone disc and both simultaneously threw a spear. The object of the game was to have one's spear land nearest to the stone. Southeastern Indians were enthusiastic gamblers, often wagering all they possessed on the outcome of the match.

Bartram describes typical domestic dwellings in some detail (see fig. 13):

> The dwellings of the Upper Creeks consist of little squares, or rather of four dwelling-houses inclosing a square area, exactly on the plan of the Public Square. Every family, however, has not four of these houses; some have but three, others not more than two, and some but one, according to the circumstances of the individual, or the number of his family. Those who have four buildings have a particular use for each building. One serves as a cook-room and winter lodging-house, another as a summer lodging-house and hall for receiving visitors, and a third for a granary or provision house, etc. The last is commonly two stories high, and divided into two apartments, transversely, the lower story of one being a potato house, for keeping such other roots and fruits as require to be kept close, or defended from cold in winter. The chamber over it is the council. At the other end of this building, both upper and lower stories are open

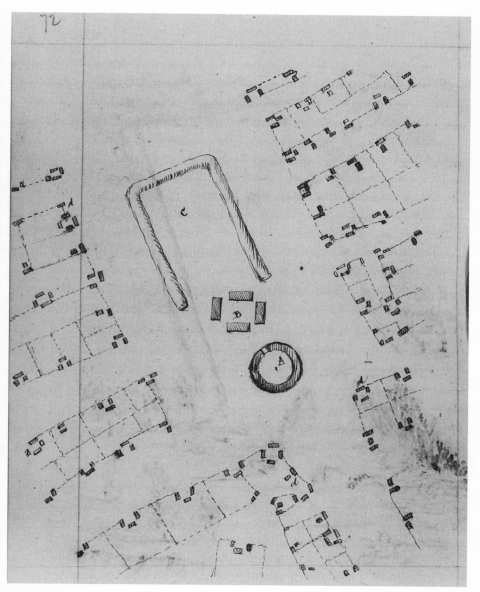

13. John Howard Payne's copy of William Bartram's "A Plan of the Muscogulge or Upper Creek Town." Reproduced courtesy of the Historical Society of Pennsylvania.

on their sides: the lower story serves for a shed for their saddles, pack-saddles, and gears, and other lumber; the loft over it is a very spacious, airy, pleasant pavilion, where the chief of the family reposes in the hot seasons, and receives his guests, etc. The fourth house (which completes the square) is a skin or ware-house, if the proprietor is a wealthy man, and engaged in trade or traffic, where he keeps his deer-skins, furs, merchandise, etc., and treats his customers. Smaller or less wealthy families make one, two, or three houses serve all their purposes as well as they can. (Bartram 1853: 54–56)

Eighteenth-century Creek towns were often dispersed over large areas, a change in settlement pattern from the more compactly organized towns of the sixteenth century. Another important shift in settlement took place: many of the towns chose to locate away from the Coosa River. They moved up several streams, particularly Talladega and Tallaseehatchee creeks. The main towns, however, did not go upstream to the ecotone location bordering the Piedmont, although the eighteenth-century component at the Sylacauga Water Works archaeological site is one exception.

Social Organization

The Creeks had a matrilineal kinship organization in which they traced kin ties through the female line. They considered only people related through their mother's blood relatives to be kin; they did not consider the father and his relatives to be blood relations. This is not to say that men were unimportant in the family structure. In such a system, a child's mother's brother (that is, an uncle) is the most important male in his family, not the father. The uncle is accepted as a blood relative; the father is not. The uncle would discipline and help the child. In turn, the child would expect to inherit from the uncle. Thus, a man had formal responsibility for his sister's children, rather than his own, although informally he no doubt looked after his children since he lived in the same household (Hudson 1976).

The Creeks recognized matrilineages, or groups of related people, who owned lands together, jointly made important decisions, and had certain ritual obligations. Everyone in a matrilineage was closely related and could explain or demonstrate genealogical connections through the female line to anyone else in the matrilineage. Creek towns, called "talwas," consisted of four to ten such matrilineages (Hudson 1976).

Above the matrilineage in size and complexity was the matrilineal clan. Clan members all believed themselves to be distantly related but could not necessarily demonstrate exactly how they were linked by specific kin ties. Each clan consisted of several matrilineages, and they identified themselves with a particular animal or natural phenomenon. While matrilineages were usually restricted to individual talwas, clans were larger and cut across talwa divisions. This system helped integrate Creek society (Hudson 1976). During the nineteenth century, after their removal to Oklahoma, clans among the Abihkutci were named Potato, Fox, Aktayatci, Woksi, Eagle, Kapitca, Skunk, Bird, Alligator, Tami, Turkey, Beaver, Bear, Panther, Wind, Deer, Wolf, Wildcat, Pahosa, Mole, and Raccoon (Swanton 1928:124).

Clans functioned to provide hospitality to travelers and to afford mutual protection and assistance. Thus, a traveling Creek sought out clan members when visiting another town. Although they might never have met before, these clanspeople always extended hospitality. If someone were killed, clans members would avenge the death, a practice that often led to blood feuds between clans. The Creeks had a vague notion that one should not kill or eat one's clan animal, but they did not closely follow this restriction (Hudson 1976). Obviously, if people of the Deer Clan had observed this prohibition, they would have risked starvation. Adair (1930:17) noted, "The Indians, however, bear no religious respect to the animals from which they derive the names of their tribes, but will kill any of the species, when opportunity serves."

There were further social divisions above the clan (fig. 14). Several clans were considered closely related and formed what anthropologists call a phratry (Swanton 1928:120). These phratries functioned to regulate marriage; people could not marry within their phratry.

Finally, at the highest level, each Creek clan belonged to one of two moieties or dual divisions. These were the Hathagalgi (white) and the Tchilokogalgi (red, or more properly "people of different speech"). Generally, the white division was considered to be the oldest in the society, while the red division consisted of newcomers to the confederacy. Little is known of the functions of the moiety. The moiety division served to de-

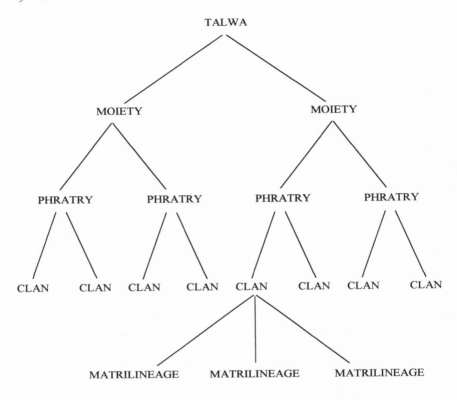

14. Creek social organization. Drawing by Julie Barnes Smith.

fine sides for practice ballgames within a town, but there is no evidence that moieties ever regulated marriage (Swanton 1928:165, 167).

Several rules controlled marriage among the Creeks. Certain people were not allowed to marry each other. The phratry, clan, and the lineage were exogamous—that is, there was a rule forbidding marriage to anyone else in one's phratry, clan, or lineage. The Creeks also frowned upon marriage to anyone in the father's clan. Marriage was an important tie between two clans, and the clan elders often made the arrangements, although they never forced anyone to marry. Following various negotiations and exchanges of gifts, the actual ceremony was simple. The man proved he could hunt by providing meat, while the woman provided vegetable food and cooked a meal. The man had to provide a house for his new wife, usually located close to her matrilineage. (This practice is known as matrilocal residence.) The house became the property of the wife. If the couple divorced, she kept the house and the children. Because children belonged to the matrilineage of their mother and the father was not considered a blood relative, he could never claim them. Divorce was not uncommon, and adultery was usually the cause (Hudson 1976). Adultery was punished by "severe flagellations and loss of hair, nose, and ears, in both parties, if they are taken" (Romans 1962:98).

Men were allowed to have more than one wife if they could afford to support them and if the first wife agreed. Such plural marriages usually joined a man with sisters since they could all live together in one household. A man who married two unrelated women would have to construct two houses. The second wife would then have to leave her matrilineage in order to live in the compound of her husband near his first wife (Hudson 1976). A man who married women unrelated to each other was asking for trouble!

At the death of a spouse, there was a four-year mourning period for men and women (Hudson 1976:201). Adair notes, "The Muskohge widows are obliged to live a chaste single life, for the tedious space of four years. . . . Their law compels the widow, through the long term of her weeks, to refrain all public company and diversions, at the penalty of an adulteress; and likewise to go with flowing hair, without the privilege of oil to anoint it. The nearest kinsmen of the deceased husband, keep a very watchful eye over her conduct, in this respect" (Adair 1930:195). A woman could not dress attractively or take care of her hair, and she had to wail every morning for a year. But there were ways of avoiding this long mourning period. The surviving spouse could remarry someone in the deceased spouse's clan. Again, this shows that marriage was really more a tie between clans than between two individuals (Hudson 1976).

The Creeks also had conventions for dealing with outsiders. Most writers noted the generous hospitality of the Creeks. Bernard Romans wrote that "they are very hospitable and never fail of making a stranger heartily welcome, offering him the pipe as soon as he arrives, while the good women are employed to prepare a dish of venison and homany, with some bread made of maize and flour, and being wrapped in maize leaves, baked under the ashes; when it is served up they accompany it with bears fat purified to a perfect chrystalline oyl, and a bottle of honey with which last article the country abounds" (Romans 1962:92).

Political Organization

The principal political unit of the eighteenth century was the "talwa," or
Creek town. The talwa consisted of a politico-religious center and a supporting population, which might be dispersed over a large area—a major
change from the compact towns of the sixteenth century. According to
Bartram, "every town and village is to be considered as an independent
nation or tribe having its Mico or Chief" (1853:220). The relationship
between the chiefdom of the sixteenth century and the talwa of the eighteenth century is not fully understood. Apparently, the simple chiefdoms
of the sixteenth century were reduced to one talwa by the eighteenth
century. Thus, following epidemics of European disease, the eight towns
of Coosa Province reported by Luna's forces probably collapsed into the
Coosa town of the eighteenth century.

Each Creek talwa was run by a "mico," or chief. Whereas the sixteenth-century paramount chief of Coosa held absolute power over his
subjects, the eighteenth-century mico was little more than a spokesman
for the town council. Bartram states, "The Mico is considered the first
man in dignity and power in the nation or town, and is the supreme civil
magistrate; yet he is, in fact, no more than president of the national council of his own tribe and town, and has no executive power independent of
the council, which is convened every day in the forenoon, and held in the
Public Square" (Bartram 1853:28).

Micos led their people more than they commanded them. The mico
dispensed food from the public granary and acted as the town's link to the
outside world. He received ambassadors and other visitors, and he often
held public feasts. He was often chosen from a particular clan (Wind
Clan). This was perhaps a reflection of the ascribed status of the earlier
ruling lineage. A mico often passed down the leadership role to his
nephew (his own clansman), but under the influence of Europeans in the
eighteenth century, there was an increasing tendency for the Mico's son
to inherit his father's position (Corkran 1967:14–15). An interpreter or
speaker, called the "yatika," assisted the mico. The yatika was known as
a great orator and often helped sway public opinion.

All adult males were members of the council, and each could express
his opinion at council meetings in the town square. It is likely, based on
the presence of large public buildings, that town councils were present in

the sixteenth century and even earlier, but they appear to have become more important (that is, more powerful politically) by the eighteenth century. Bernard Romans, a firsthand observer, compared the town square with the Roman forum (Romans 1962:93). The council would discuss important decisions until it reached a consensus.

Although there were no social classes among the eighteenth-century Upper Creeks, men could be ranked according to their achievements in warfare and their hunting prowess. Religious and medical practitioners could also achieve relatively high social status. Men worked hard to achieve rank, and they were proud of the emblems of their status. These included tattoos, special names, and special seats in the council house (Hudson 1976).

The council of adult males had several subdivisions, including the "heniha" or Second Men, Beloved Old Men, and several grades of warriors. The heniha were chosen to oversee public works and internal affairs, often serving as advisors to the mico. The Beloved Old Men were distinguished elders who had served the talwa as warriors or as heniha in the past and were valued for their wisdom. They were often the elders of their clans, and the mico valued their advice above that of the Second Men.

The grades of warriors consisted of war chiefs (tastanagi), big warriors, and little warriors. Their leader was the Great Warrior. The Great Warrior had a war speaker who acted as his spokesman, much as the yatika aided the mico. The war speaker was often the greatest orator of the town. Warriors fought their enemies and also played the ballgame called "the younger brother of war." This extremely violent game, played against other towns, often resulted in the death of one or more participants. Although the Indians staked many large wagers on the outcome, the contest was more than just a game. It had important political functions and often served to define relationships between towns (Hudson 1976).

There were other political divisions above the talwa. One grouping was known to the Europeans as "the Abihkas." As used by Europeans, this term included all towns on the Coosa River above the junction with the Tallapoosa. It also included towns on the middle reaches of the Tallapoosa River. The origin of this grouping of the towns is not clear. It may have been rooted in aboriginal practice, or simply imposed by Europeans for their own purposes. Such a system would have been useful in making treaties. In one sense, the eighteenth-century Abihkas appear to have been the remnants of the sixteenth-century Coosa Paramount Chiefdom that settled on the Coosa and Tallapoosa rivers.

The Coosa-Abihka people, in the narrow sense used in this study, were part of the Creeks in general. They were defined by linguistic as well as political and cultural terms. The Creeks were divided into the Upper Creeks and the Lower Creeks, a level of organization above and separate from the red (Tchilokogalgi) and white (Hathagalgi) moiety divisions of towns (fig. 15).

Upper Creeks included (1) the Coosa-Abihka peoples on the Coosa River and its tributaries (the people who are the subject of this work), (2) the Okfuskee towns on the upper Tallapoosa River, who were closely related to the Coosa-Abihkas (indeed these groups were often lumped together as Abihkas in the eighteenth century by literate Europeans), (3) the Alabamas located near the junction of the Coosa and Tallapoosa rivers near modern Montgomery, Alabama, and finally, (4) the Tallapoosas proper, a group of towns on the lower Tallapoosa River. The Alabamas included people who had apparently been in present-day eastern Mississippi in de Soto's day. They were thus newcomers and were joined by the Napochies and the Koasatis from eastern Tennessee in the late seventeenth and early eighteenth centuries.

The Alabama-Koasati alliance probably came about when both groups moved to the area of the Coosa-Tallapoosa River junction. The Okfuskees were apparently related to the Coosa people, according to research by John Swanton (1928), but their prehistory is poorly known. The Tallapoosas appear to have been largely in place on the lower Tallapoosa River at least by the beginning of the seventeenth century, if not before. Various refugee groups joined them to increase their population. Indeed, some of the Coosa group appear to have moved in with the Tallapoosas at one time, indicating their close connection.

The Lower Creeks consisted of those towns on the Chattahoochee and Flint rivers in present-day Georgia and Alabama. While several of these towns had a long history in the area, undoubtedly going back into prehistory, other towns were recent arrivals. It is of interest to our story that the town of Chiaha appears in this area—apparently the same Chiaha that de Soto and Pardo found in the upper east Tennessee area in the sixteenth

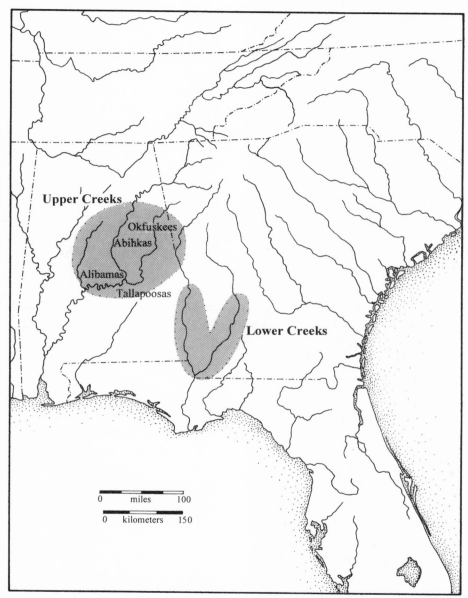

Upper Creeks

Okfuskees

Abihkas

Alibamas

Tallapoosas

Lower Creeks

0   miles   100

0   kilometers   150

15. Creek divisions. Map by Julie Barnes Smith.

century. Similarly, the Uchi also settled with the Lower Creeks, but Pardo found them allied with eastern Tennessee towns (and supposedly living in that region) in the 1560s.

All the Creeks and their close allies had formed an overall alliance, the Creek Confederacy, by the eighteenth century. It is likely that the confederacy grew out of efforts to deal with European powers. Indeed, the Creeks became quite adept at manipulating English, French, and Spanish interests for their benefit, often engaging in trade and receiving presents from each (Corkran 1967).

The origin of the Creek Confederacy would be an excellent topic of study in its own right (see Knight 1994), but a few words are in order here. Elsewhere I have argued that the formation of the confederacy was a gradual process (Smith 1987). It began as the chiefdoms broke up and towns amalgamated to maintain a viable population in the late sixteenth and early seventeenth centuries. Population movements, such as those described in chapter 6 for the Coosa-Abihka, forced new groups into contact. Pressure from armed northern Indians and slave raiders, both European and their native allies, forced other movements to take place in the late seventeenth century. The Spaniard Marcos Delgado noted such movements in 1686 when he reported the Koasati and other northern groups had settled near the junction of the Coosa and Tallapoosa rivers.

In 1690, many Creek towns moved east to the Ocmulgee and Oconee rivers in present-day Georgia to be nearer to the English trade. This cluster of towns in Georgia undoubtedly began efforts at cooperation. Indeed, William Bartram recorded a Creek legend that the confederacy was formed at Ocmulgee town in central Georgia at that time. However, Frank Schnell (1989) has argued that the confederacy was born on the Chattahoochee River slightly earlier.

The Yamassee War of 1715 was a revolt of many southeastern Indian groups against unfair trading practices of English traders and overwhelming culture changes in general. The war also brought many of the Muskogee groups into closer contact, and they cooperated on an unprecedented scale. By the early eighteenth century, Europeans began to speak of the Creek Confederacy. During the period 1715–1738, one of the most important leaders in the confederacy, the Abihka mico Hobohatchey, appeared to speak for many of the Upper Creeks (Corkran 1967).

Abihka, an important cornerstone of the Creek Confederacy, was regarded as one of the four "foundation towns." It was the head peace town of the Upper Creeks. Peace towns were old towns from which daughter towns had split off and were important places where disputes were settled (Hudson 1976:238) as opposed to a war town—a new town in the confederacy. The Abihkas were also known as "the door shutters" because of their position as the gateway to the Creeks for their northern enemies, the Cherokee (Swanton 1928:307).

While the Creek Confederacy was important, it must not be confused with the sixteenth-century paramount chiefdom. Ethnohistorian John Swanton misinterpreted the political relationships of the sixteenth-century towns as forerunners of the confederacy (1928:310). In reality, they were entirely different structures. The paramount chiefdom was ruled by a semi-divine chief with great authority to demand tribute and fight wars. In contrast, the confederacy was an alliance of basically independent groups who cooperated when it served their purposes in dealing with Europeans. The paramount chiefdom had been much more centralized than the eighteenth-century confederacy.

Warfare

Bernard Romans described the Creeks in general as having "an indefatigable thirst for blood" and as being "truly politicians bred, and so very jealous of their lands, that they will not only not part with any, but endeavour constantly to enlarge their territories by conquest and claiming large tracts from the Cherokees and Chactaws" (Romans 1962:91). Revenge was often the principal motive for war. French and English records describe frequent wars with the Choctaws and the Cherokee during the eighteenth century, and conflicts with Europeans were constant. Warfare was a means to achieve high social status and was thus important to social mobility. James Adair notes, "They are so extremely anxious to be distinguished by high war-titles, that sometimes a small party of warriors, on failing of success in their campaign, have been detected in murdering some of their own people, for sake of their scalps" (Adair 1930:276).

Warfare was conducted in groups that ranged from three warriors up to dozens. By the eighteenth century, firearms were important in warfare, but the use of bows and arrows continued. Another important weapon was the atasa, or war club. This was a gunstock-shaped wooden object about two feet long, with a metal point driven in near the end. The atasa was the symbol of war.

Many complex rituals were associated with warfare, and the ritual purity of the warriors was particularly important for the raid to be successful. In the eighteenth century, warfare was virtually never for the conquest of lands or to bring in tribute (probable sixteenth-century motives). It was primarily for revenge for slain clans members and for glory and therefore social advancement.

Religion

The principal Creek deity was the Master of Breath, who was closely related to the Sun. The earthly representative of the Master of Breath was the sacred fire, kept burning in the rotunda or square ground. This fire had to be kept pure by avoiding contamination by such substances as urine, saliva, or any food with saliva on it. It was a special fire constructed of four logs in a cross shape or a spiral of small crossed sticks. This fire was carefully tended and never allowed to go out during the year. At the principal ceremony of the year, the Green Corn Ceremony or busk, the sacred fire was extinguished and a new fire built, symbolically purifying the entire town. At the busk all crimes except murder were forgiven, and thanks were offered for the crops, wild food, and wild game. The ceremony served to preserve the tribal health, forge social solidarity, and insure fertility of wild and domesticated plants and animals (Hudson 1976). This ceremony was held in the summer or early fall, when the new corn crop was ready for the harvest.

The moon was another important deity and was related to the sun. It was associated with rain and menstruation and with fertility in general. Thunder was also an important deity.

The Creeks viewed the world as a large square island surrounded by water, with a solid dome of sky over all. The sun and moon passed around the world under the dome of the sky. Above the sky dome was the Upper World, a place where supernatural forms of animals lived. It epitomized order and regularity (Hudson 1976).

Below the island world and the waters was the Under World, which epitomized fertility, disorder, and change. It was also the home of various supernatural creatures, such as the Tie Snake. The Tie Snake was very powerful and might carry people away. It could also control rain. There was also a Sharp-Breasted Snake, who was responsible for the marks made by lightning. Finally there was the Horned Snake, who aided heroes.

There was also a spirit realm, where the spirits of the deceased went. Those who had followed an upright life traveled along the Milky Way to the land of the blessed (Hudson 1976). Treatment of the dead was thus important to the Creeks. Romans notes, "The dead are buried in a sitting posture, and they are furnished with a musket, powder, and ball, a hatchet, pipe, some tobacco, a club, a bow and arrows, a looking glass, some vermillion and other trinkets, in order to come well provided in the world of spirits" (Romans 1962:98–99). Historical sources remain silent on burial practices for women.

James Adair mentions a carved wooden statue in human form that belonged to the head war town of the upper Muskogee country. He believed that it perpetuated the memory of some distinguished hero. This statue apparently was a vestige of those found in Mississippian prehistoric archaeological sites, such as Etowah. Knight (1986) suggests that such images were part of an ancestor cult. It is probable that they symbolized the mythical founding ancestors of the towns. Adair apparently viewed one of the last vestiges of this aspect of Mississippian religion during the eighteenth century.

The statue was served the first shell dipperful of black drink. This was a ritually purifying emetic beverage brewed from the leaves of the *Ilex vomitoria* holly. Black drink contained caffeine and was served before any important deliberation by the council (Hudson 1979).

Like many other southeastern Indians, the Creeks had a belief in a race of little people—dwarfs or fairies—who could endow humans with supernatural powers. One of the most powerful charms was the sabia, a lustrous crystal believed to be the product of a plant. The sabia allowed a man to gain control over deer and women.

There were various types of religious specialists, including Fasting Men (doctors) and Prophets. Fasting Men were taught by accomplished doctors. They went on a vision quest to learn how to cure illness. Other shamans controlled the weather, which was particularly important to these agricultural people. Prophets were the younger of twins. They were born with the power to see the future and to diagnose disease (Hudson 1976). Bartram notes that there was an ancient high priest, "a person of great power and consequence in the state." His word in the council was very important (Bartram 1853:24).

Disease was believed to be caused by animals, birds, fish, and spirits of the dead. Plants supplied medicines to cure illnesses, and various formulas were spoken as part of the cure. There was also a belief in witchcraft. Adair states, "There are not greater bigots in Europe, nor persons more superstitious, than the Indians, (especially the women) concerning the power of witches, wizards, and evil spirits" (1930:38). Witches could cause illness by stealing one's soul or by injecting foreign objects into the body. Also, they could change their form, often becoming owls. Plant remedies could cure witchcraft illness, while the doctor magically sucked out foreign objects. The Cherokee, Natchez, and Chickasaw executed witches (Hudson 1976). It is likely the Creeks did also.

The Creeks were obsessed with the notion of ritual purity. People who did not follow all the rules of society became polluted. Such a person was a threat to everyone else. Comrades in war were at risk if one of the warriors was impure, so much ritual accompanied preparations for war. The ballgame was treated much as war; there were many rituals to achieve purity before the game, including the taking of black drink. Disease could erupt if people did not maintain purity. There were many rules separating warriors and menstruating women from the rest of society (Hudson 1976).

Subsistence and the Division of Labor

The Creeks had a strict division of labor that probably existed for centuries before European contact. Women did the agricultural work (except the heavy field clearing), wove baskets and made pottery, tanned hides, and looked after children (often with the aid of the elderly of either sex). Domesticated sunflower and other seed crops supplemented the corn, beans, and squash that were grown in fields just outside the town. By the eighteenth century, some European-introduced crops, such as peaches and watermelon, were important in the economy. Bartram notes that some apples were also grown among Creeks in general (1853:48), but it is unclear if they were present in the Coosa-Abihka territory. Women also collected wild foods, including various fruits, nuts, and berries. Adair notes that the men helped in planting before they went off to war (1930:276), but in general farming was a female occupation.

Men provided meat by hunting, traded for European goods, and participated in war. By the eighteenth century, firearms were important in hunting and warfare, but the bow and arrow continued in use throughout the century. Small brass triangular or conical points replaced stone arrow points. Deer, bear, and turkey were the principal sources of meat, although many other small animals were taken. Fishing was also important, as Adair noted for all the southeastern Indians in general. Cattle, chickens, horses, and pigs grew in importance during the eighteenth century. In speaking of the Creeks in general, Bernard Romans mentions small cattle, hogs, turkeys, ducks, dunghill fowls, and horses (Romans 1962:93, 94). Europeans found the Creek men to be lazy by their standards, spending much time smoking and discussing affairs of state in the rotunda or square ground. However, we must remember that the men had dangerous occupations, going out to hunt and to take part in war.

Dress and Ornamentation

Adair gives a lengthy description of Creek dress of the eighteenth century. Men wore breechcloths, and women wore skin or Stroud cloth (wool) wrapped skirts, fastened with a leather belt "commonly covered with brass runners or buckles. But this sort of loose petticoat, reaches only to their hams, in order to shew their exquisitely fine proportioned limbs." In the winter either sex might wear buffalo robes. Men usually went barefooted and always went bareheaded, but when hunting they wore deerskin boots that reached up high on their thighs. These might be ornamented with fawn's trotters (dewclaws), small pieces of tinkling metal, or wild-turkey cockspurs.

Both sexes often wrapped a piece of cloth around themselves, like a Roman toga. James Adair observed, "The men fasten several different sorts of beautiful feathers, frequently in tufts; or the wing of a red bird, or the skin of a small hawk, to a lock of hair on the crown of their heads. And every different Indian nation when at war, trim their hair, after a different manner, through contempt of each other; thus we can distinguish an enemy in the woods, so far off as we can see him" (1930:9).

Many of the old men wore a long wide frock made of skins. "They formerly wore shirts, made of drest deer skins, for their summer visiting dress: but their winter-hunting clothes were long and shaggy, made of the skins of panthers, bucks, bears, beavers, and otters; the fleshy sides outward, sometimes doubled, and always softened like velvet-cloth, though they retained their fur and hair" (Adair 1930:7–8).

The southeastern Indians in general were fond of glass beads obtained from the European traders. Adair notes that they were used in garters, sashes, necklaces, and bracelets, worn on the crown of the head, and sometimes tied to the cartilage of the nose (1930:178). Silver jewelry obtained from European traders, particularly ear bobs, bracelets, and gorgets, were also in use in his day.

Bartram noted that the Creek Micos were tattooed with a variety of bluish colored designs, including depictions of the sun, moon, and planets. Zones or belts of scrolls divided the body into panels that contained various scenes, which included wild game, landscapes, battle scenes, and "a thousand other fancies" (Bartram 1853:19). He also noted the use of bear's oil and ground sumac berries as a hair dressing (1853:30).

Romans described dance "stockings" (leggings) of the women, made of leather and adorned with hundreds of dewclaws to make sounds "like that of the Castagnettes" (1962:95). Dewclaws were also used in earrings and bracelets. He went on to note, "The men are also very fond of dress; my guide across the Peninsula, employed above two hours at his toilet, at Mr. Mountrie's house, four miles from St. Augustine, before he would venture to show himself in town" (Romans 1962:96).

The Archaeology and Ethnohistory of Eighteenth-Century Coosa-Abihka

During the early eighteenth century, the main town of Coosa was at the Childersburg site (DeJarnette and Hansen 1960). The identification of the archaeological site with the historically known town is certain; many eighteenth-century maps clearly place Coosa at this location. The Childersburg site is on a high terrace overlooking the confluence of Talladega Creek with the Coosa River in Talladega County, Alabama (fig. 16). The site covers an area of 450 by 500 feet (2.1 ha). Excavation of a portion of the site exposed twelve burials and ninety-five features. While postholes

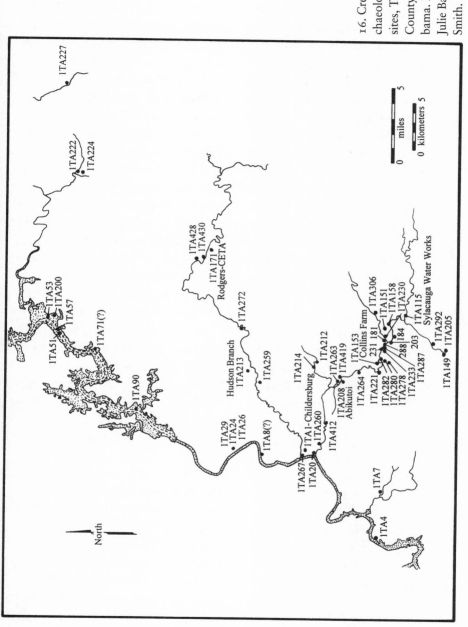

16. Creek archaeological sites, Talladega County, Alabama. Map by Julie Barnes Smith.

were recorded, no structures were recognized in DeJarnette and Hansen's report. However, possibly one or more structures were present and represented by burial clusters and postholes. Assuming there was a structure present, it was of the ground-level, summer structure type recognized on the Tallapoosa River drainage in contemporary Creek Indian sites. Waselkov (1990) has argued that construction of semi-subterranean winter houses ceased about A.D. 1700, perhaps because most of the people were seasonally dispersed while they hunted deer for the skin trade.

European grave goods typically accompanied burials at the site. Glass beads were popular, as were brass buttons (probably representing European coats, based on their position in one burial), brass buckles with belt fragments, and brass keepers. Also found were iron knives, European clay pipes, brass tinkling cones, a brass finger ring, brass wire bracelets, gun flints, musket balls, and a complete early eighteenth-century French trade gun. This occurrence is the first in the Coosa River sequence where complete guns were found among grave goods and European clothing was present in some quantity. Late burials at the site contained silver jewelry and glass beads of the types traded in the last half of the eighteenth century.

Aboriginal grave goods were also present but in more limited quantities. Only five of the twelve burials contained aboriginal grave goods. Two of these contained only cane mats, more likely to have been burial wrappings than goods for the afterlife. Other graves included a flint projectile point found with an adult and a pottery pipe found with an adult male. Beads made from the central whorl of a large whelk shell were found with a child. No pottery vessels were found in graves, in contrast to earlier sites in the region. Changes in their culture were rapidly making the Creeks more and more dependent on European goods.

Archaeological features at the Childersburg site included fifty-two midden pits, fifteen postholes, twenty-two smudge pits filled with charred corn cobs (for hide smoking or insect control), four fire pits, and two elongated pits or trenches. Although Childersburg was excavated before the introduction of flotation techniques, some plant remains were reported. Cultigens included corn, peaches (an Old World introduction), and squash, while wild plant remains included hickory nut and cane. Further analysis by Elisabeth Sheldon (1982) adds possible beans and walnuts to the list. Sheldon notes that the maize is of the Northern Flint variety and occurred in cobs of 7, 8 (36 percent), 9, 10 (46 percent), 11, 12 (14 percent), 13, and 14 rows (4 percent). Eggshell was reported, signifying the presence of introduced domesticated chickens. Faunal remains were not analyzed. However, by the end of the eighteenth century, the Creeks were using domesticated cattle and pigs in addition to wild deer, bear, and turkey.

There are several historic accounts of Coosa in the eighteenth century, and the town appears on several maps. One of these is the William Bonar map of 1757 (fig. 17). James Adair, an eyewitness, described Coosa as follows: "in the upper or most western part of the country of the Muskohge, there was an old beloved town, now reduced to a small ruinous village, called Koosah, which is still a place of safety for those who kill undesignedly. It stands on commanding ground, over-looking a bold river, which after running about forty leagues, sweeps close by the late mischievous French garrison Alebamah, and down to Mobille-Sound, 200 leagues distance, and so into the gulph of Florida" (1930:166). Adair was clearly describing the Childersburg site, based on his description of its commanding location. This description was made sometime after his Alebamah French garrison, Fort Toulouse, was abandoned in 1763, but before the publication of his *History of the American Indians* in 1775.

David Taitt described Coosa in 1772 as "Coosa Old Town," saying that it was mostly grown over (Mereness 1916:534). He stated that people from Tallassiehatchie, a small town nearby, were moving into the old town site. Thus apparently the town was revitalized for a time in the early 1770s. William Bartram visited Coosa in 1775 and described the town as half deserted and in ruins (Gatschet 1901:402). Clearly by the mid-1770s, Coosa had lost much of its former importance. Benjamin Hawkins (1848: 39) describes the town in 1799 as follows:

> Coo-sau on the left bank of Coo-sau, between two creeks Eu-fau-lau and Nau-chee. The town borders on the first, above, and on the other river. The town is on a high and beautiful hill; the land on the river is rich and flat for two hundred yards, then waving and rich, fine for wheat and corn. It is a limestone country, with fine springs, and a very desirable one; there is reed on the branches, and peavine in the rich bottoms and hill sides, moss in the river and on the rock beds of the creek. They get fish plentifully in the spring season, near the mouth of Eu-fau-lau-hat-che; they are rock, trout, buffalo, red

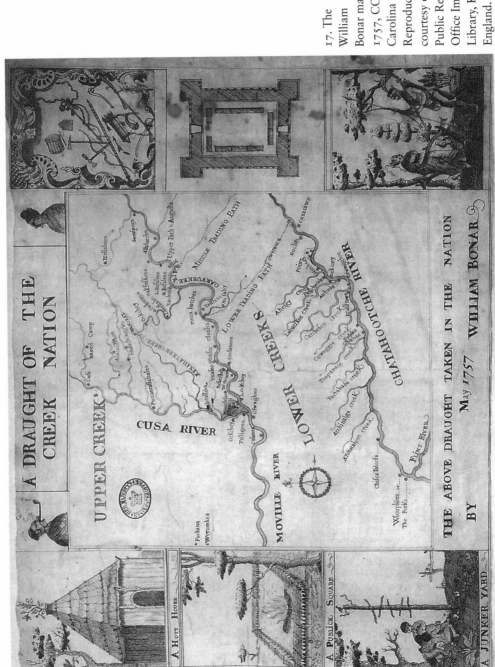

17. The William Bonar map, 1757, CO 700 Carolina 21. Reproduced courtesy of the Public Record Office Image Library, Kew, England.

horse, and perch. They have fine stocks of horses, hogs, and cattle; the town gives name to the river and is sixty miles above Tus-kee-gee.

There are various estimates of Coosa population. In the 1738 Spanish census, Coosa is said to have had 100 warriors and the Coosa group of towns had 414. In 1750 the French estimated the same populations at 30-plus and 240-plus, respectively. In 1760 there were 430 men in all the Coosa towns; in 1761, there were 270 "hunters" (Swanton 1946:126). Assuming four or five residents per warrior, the 1760 population of the Coosa town group was about 1,720–2,150 people.

Antoine S. Le Page du Pratz, a Frenchman, had the following to say about the Abeikas and "Conchacs" or Coosas: "To the north of the Ali-bamous are the Abeikas and Conchacs, who, as far as I can learn, are the same people; yet the name of Conchac seems appropriated to one part more than another. They are situated at a distance from the great rivers, and consequently have no large canes in their territory. The canes that grow among them are not thicker than one's finger, and are at the same time so very hard, that when they are split, they cut like knives, which these people call conchacs. The language of this nation is almost the same with that of the Chicasaws, in which the word conchac signifies a knife" (du Pratz 1774:307–8).

By the middle eighteenth century, the principal town of the middle Coosa River area was known as Abihkutci, or "Little Abihka." This suggests that it was a daughter town split off from the earlier main town of Abihka. Perhaps the late seventeenth-century Woods Island site (see chapter 6) represents an amalgam of Coosa and Abihka populations, known as Abihka. Then in the early eighteenth century, following the Yamassee War (1715) or War of the Cherokee (1716), the Coosa River people again moved south to establish separate towns of Abihkutci and Coosa. The town of Abihkutci was located at the Bead Field site, 1Ta208 (Knight, Cole, and Walling 1984:115) and its vicinity. Several historic Indian sites are known in this area, and it is likely that Abihkutci was a very dispersed settlement (see fig. 16). Although this site underwent some excavation in the 1960s, the work was never reported and the collections have not been located.

Abihka was an important white or peace town among the eighteenth-century Upper Creeks (Gatschet 1901:387). While Apica had been a minor town in the paramount chiefdom of Coosa in the sixteenth century, by the early eighteenth century it had eclipsed Coosa in importance. A town list prepared in 1700 by the Frenchman Charles Levasseur includes "Apicales" (Knight and Adams 1981). On many maps and in many accounts, the towns on the Coosa River in the Childersburg area are known as the Abihkas. Daniel Coxe stated in 1741, "the Becaes or Abecaes have thirteen towns" (Gatschet 1901:390). Gatschet (1901:391) places Abihkutci on Tallahatchee Creek, five miles from the Coosa River. This location corresponds to a cluster of archaeological sites: 1Ta208, 1Ta263, and 1Ta419 (fig. 16) and to the location on the Bonar map of 1757 (fig. 17).

Swanton (1946:82) assembles population figures from several historic sources (for numbers of gunmen or warriors) for Abihkutci town as follows: for 1738, 30; 1750, 60-plus; 1760, 130; 1761, 50; 1772, 45. Again assuming four or five inhabitants per warrior, the Abihkutci population was about 200–300 people.

In 1725, a Captain Fitch journeyed to the Creeks and mentions sixty headmen representing twenty towns of the Abecas and Upper Tallappoop's (Tallapoosas) (Mereness 1916:179). This account clearly includes people living on the upper Tallapoosa—probably the Okfuskee towns, and Swanton (1922) states that the Okfuskee were originally part of the Coosa group. Fitch also mentions war with the Cherokee and Chickasaw (Mereness 1916:202). Benoit reports that the war with the Cherokee had ended by 1732 (Rowland, Sanders, and Galloway 1984a:120). In 1725 the "Abihkas" traded 8,000 skins to the French (Surrey 1916:348), but this term probably includes most of the Coosa and upper Tallapoosa towns. During the 1710s an important "king" or "mico," Hobohatchey, gained control of the Abihkas. He was important as a staunch English supporter in Creek Confederacy affairs until about 1738 (Corkran 1967).

By 1744, the Abihkas had their own resident English trader. Lachlan McGillivray traded for the English for many years, and helped secure the Abihkas to the English cause. Although there were pro-French factions from time to time, the Abihkas largely remained loyal to the British interests. Their town was on the trading path to the Chickasaws, and many British traders passed through it. The French were never able to supply as many trade goods as the British and simply could not compete with them.

In 1746, M. de Beauchamp mentions Abikudshi Abihkas in his journal (Rowland, Sanders, and Galloway 1984a:289). He fails to mention the Coosa, again suggesting that the Abihkas were the most prominent group at the time. Records in the French archives mention the Abihkas' war with the Choctaws in the 1750s (Rowland, Sanders, and Galloway 1984b: 78). At this time, the Abihkas were allied with the Tallapoosas, a Creek group of towns on the lower Tallapoosa River. There was great fear among the French due to the influence of English traders among the Abihkas (Rowland, Sanders, and Galloway 1984b:20). In 1749 the Abihkas, in alliance with the Chickasaws, attacked the Arkansas (Rowland, Sanders, and Galloway 1984b:34). In 1758 Kerlérec reports that the emperor of the Kawitas (a Lower Creek town on the Chattahoochee River) assured him that the Abihka, Tallapoosa, and Alabama nations were subordinate to him. This was undoubtedly an exaggeration, although all were part of the Creek Confederacy. At this time, the "Abikudshis" were seeking peace with the French after their wars with the Choctaw (Rowland, Sanders, and Galloway 1984b:196).

In 1764 the French listed the Indian towns. One of the major divisions of Creek villages was the Abekas, and sixteen towns are listed. This list gives us a good indication of which towns the French considered to be Abihkas. "Abekoutches" and "Conchus" (Coosa?) from our present study area are listed, but so is virtually every town on the Coosa River down to the junction with the Tallapoosa River. Other towns are also listed, such as the Akfaches (Okfuskees) on the upper Tallapoosa. There is an apparent problem with too many historically documented towns compared to the archaeological site concentration in the present Talladega County area. However, if we project the concept of the Abihkas back to the 1715 town counts, this explains the discrepancy. The French considered many additional towns in their Abihka division besides the remnants of Coosa that we are considering here. The location of these towns is certain. Only Abekoutches and Conchus are located twenty-five leagues from Fort Toulouse in our area of concern. The other towns range from eighteen leagues (Petlako) to only three leagues (Petustatetchis) (Rowland 1911:95) from the fort, well south of the Coosas and Abikutchis.

Refugee Groups

During the eighteenth century, many refugee groups settled with the Upper Creek Coosa-Abihka division. In 1744 Chickasaw refugees joined the Coosa-Abihka group in the area of Talladega County, Alabama, founding what was known to the English as Breed Town (Corkran 1967:114). According to James Adair, they settled a town, Ooe-asa, somewhere on the upper Coosa. It is assumed that this is the native name for Breed Town, although it could refer to a separate settlement.

On the Mitchell map of 1755, Chickasaws are located near the headwaters of the creek that empties into the Coosa River at Coosa town. This creek must be Talladega Creek. Breed Camp is prominently shown on the Bonar map of 1757 (fig. 17) in the same location. Swanton is of the impression that this town could not have lasted long. However, he notes that David Taitt in 1772 speaks of returning Chickasaw who settled on "Caimulga Creek" about fifteen miles north from the Natchez town (Mereness 1916:532). According to the Purcell map of circa 1770, "Kaimulgee R." was the old name for Talladega Creek. Further, the modern settlement of Kymulga, Alabama, is located on Talladega Creek. Thus we may be certain that the Chickasaw settled on what is today called Talladega Creek. The cluster of historic sites, 1Ta428, 1Ta430, and 1Ta171 (fig. 16) may represent the Chickasaw settlement.

Little is known of this group, but in 1752 a white trader was killed in their town. The Creek Confederacy demanded the execution of the murderer to preserve peace with the English. Although the murderer, a young man, refused to die, his uncle committed suicide to spare the young man's life and to satisfy his clan's obligation to the confederacy (Corkran 1967: 159). (To the Creeks, the death of anyone in the murderer's clan would satisfy the need for vengeance.)

Refugee Natchez from the Mississippi Valley joined the Coosa-Abihka group in the area in the mid-eighteenth century. They settled on Tallaseehatchee Creek near the Abihkas, and intermarried extensively. Vaudreuil reports in 1750 "there are still twenty or thirty Natchez [who have] taken refuge at the Abikudshis, who recently sent me a request to receive them with favor" (Rowland, Sanders, and Galloway 1984b:49).

The census of 1760 gives a population of twenty men (Swanton 1922: 436). David Taitt visited the Natchez in 1772 and credited them with

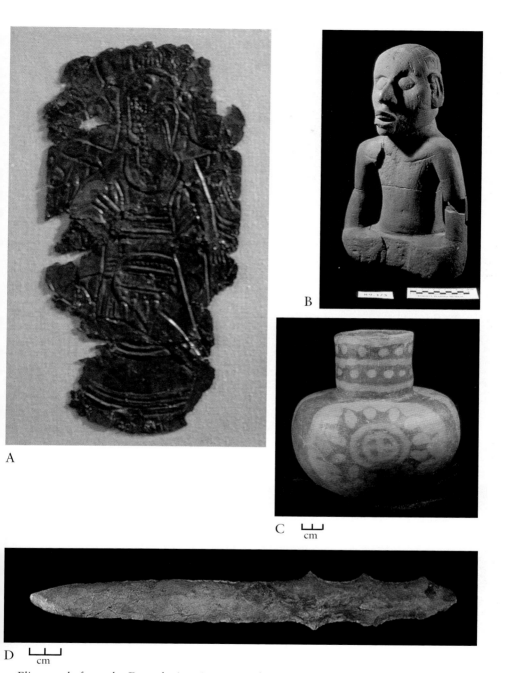

1. Elite goods from the Etowah site. *A*, copper plate; *B*, stone image; *C*, negative painted vessel; *D*, flint knife. Copyright Robert S. Peabody Museum of Archaeology, Phillips Academy, Andover, Massachusetts. All rights reserved. Reproduced with permission.

A

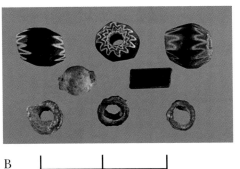

B

2. Coosawattee Valley European trade goods. *A*, copper plate; *B*, chevron beads, Poarch Farm; *C*, crossbow point, Leake site; *D*, Clarkesdale bell, Little Egypt site. Photos courtesy Richard T. Bryant.

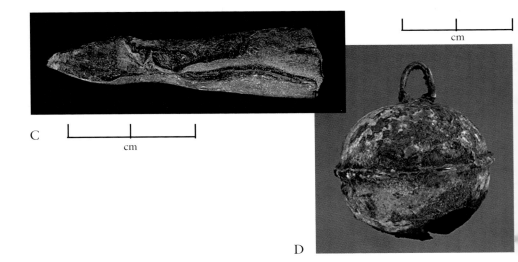

C

D

A

B

3. King site. *A*. King site sword, photo courtesy Richard Polhemus; *B*, "Piachi, Village in the Coosa Chiefdom," painting by Kenneth Townsend, reproduced courtesy of the National Park Service.

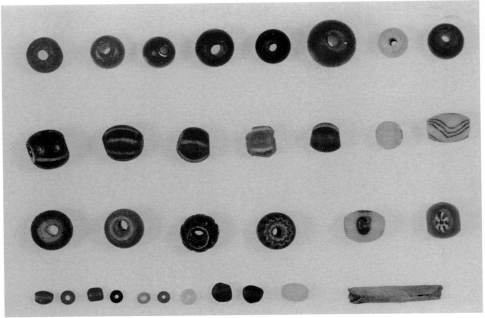

A

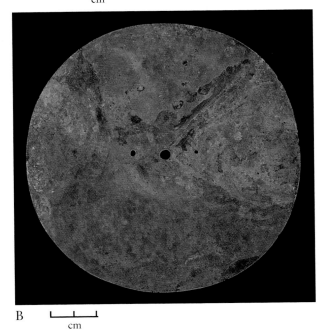

B

4. Weiss phase European artifacts. *A*, glass beads, photo courtesy Gordon L. Hight; *B*, brass disk, Seven Springs site, photo courtesy Julie Barnes Smith.

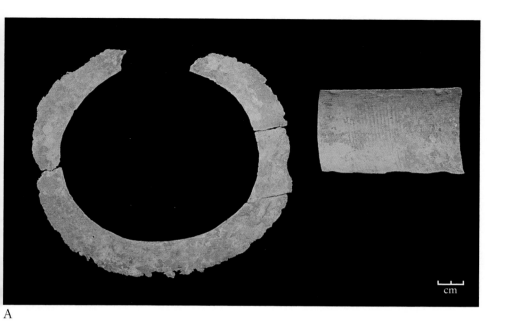

A

B

5. Gadsden area European artifacts. *A*, brass neck collar and armband, Milner Village site, photo courtesy Julie Barnes Smith; *B*, brass harness bells, Cooper Farm site, photo courtesy Gordon L. Hight.

A

cm

B

6. Gadsden area artifacts. *A*, stone pipes, Milner Village site, photo courtesy Julie Barnes Smith; *B*, Jack Greer holding Tukabatchee plate, photo courtesy of Jack Greer, photo by John A. Ritch.

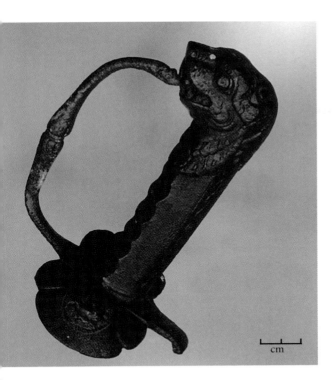

7. European artifacts from Woods Island. *A*, sword; *B*, glass beads. Photos courtesy Julie Barnes Smith.

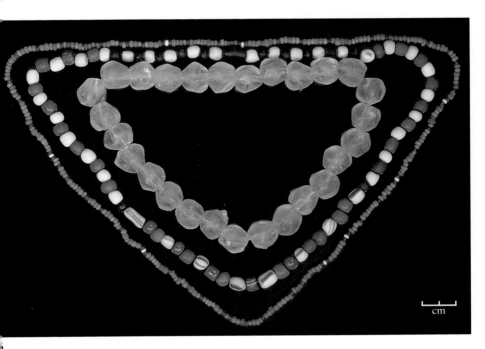

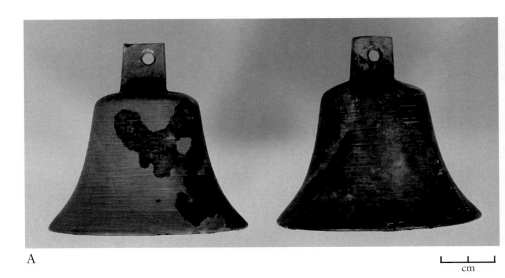

A

cm

B

cm

8. Woods Island artifacts. *A*, brass bells; *B*, iron hoe. Photos courtesy Julie Barnes Smith.

having thirty gunmen; he stated that their trader was a Mr. Cuzens (Mereness 1916:531–33). Knight (Knight, Cole, and Walling 1984) reports local opinion that the Collins Farm archaeological site on Tallaseehatchee Creek may be the Natchez settlement. This area corresponds well with the location of the "Natchi" on the Purcell map of circa 1770 (reproduced in Swanton 1922). Gatschet (1901:404) notes that the Natchez town was five miles above Abihkutci at the fork in the stream. He describes it as being scattered for two miles along the creek. There is a fork some distance east of the Collins Farm site with many eighteenth-century archaeological sites in the area and another fork near the Sylacauga Water Works site (fig. 16), which is approximately five miles from the presumed location of Abihkutci, the site 1Ta208 area. However, as we shall see, there is another possible identification of this site.

The Shawnee also settled among the Coosa-Abihka groups in 1744 (Corkran 1967:114). Vaudreuil reports their presence in 1750 at "a place called the Abikudshis" (Rowland, Sanders, and Galloway 1984b:48). James Adair mentions Shawnee who settled between the Ooe-asa and Koosah towns (Adair 1930:163). In 1752 there was a Shawnee town near the Abihka Indians. This town was apparently known by the name "Cayomulgi" (Swanton 1922:319), from which the present settlement of Kymulga, Alabama, received its name. Sites 1Ta213 and 1Ta259 are in this general area. The French census of 1760 lists a Shawnee town called Chalakagay, which Swanton (1922:319) believed might be the same word as Sylacauga. This town is said to have had fifty men. The Sylacauga Water Works archaeological site has an appropriate late eighteenth-century occupation and may represent this late site.

The Shawnee came from the Ohio River area, where they had had dealings with the French. They became staunch French supporters among the Upper Creeks (Corkran 1967). An important leader of these people on the upper Coosa was Peter Chartier, half-Shawnee and half-French and said to have come into the Creek territory in 1748 (Corkran 1967: 166, 181). Apparently there were multiple waves of Shawnee migration into the Upper Creek territory (1744 and 1748).

Other archaeological sites are known from survey work by Vernon Knight (Knight 1985b; Knight, Cole, and Walling 1984) and research by Gregory Waselkov (1980). The distribution of these sites in the Talladega County area is shown in figure 16. The vast majority of these sites are small farmsteads, and the sites shown probably range in date from the mid-seventeenth to the early nineteenth century. We know that they date from the period following European contact, but they cannot be accurately dated with present information. For these reasons it is difficult to characterize the late settlement system. The dispersed nature of the settlement is noteworthy. It can be seen that the maximum polity size for the Coosa-Abihka at this time was about 42 km in diameter. If one includes only site locations that are definitely eighteenth century and that correspond to eighteenth-century sites shown on period maps (that is, those sites on Talladega and Tallaseehatchee Creeks), the diameter of the cluster is approximately 25 km. This figure more nearly approximates the area occupied in earlier periods (see chapters 5 and 6).

Other towns of the original Coosa Paramount Chiefdom of the sixteenth century can be traced with some certainty, while others ceased to exist in the historic record. Towns that disappeared include Ulibahali, Piachi, Tali, Itaba, and Talimachusy. Many of the surviving towns relocated on the Coosa River but often some distance from the Coosa-Abihka town cluster. The towns that can be identified on the Coosa drainage in the seventeenth or eighteenth century are briefly discussed.

Other Towns of the Old Paramount Chiefdom

Napochies

Following the Tristán de Luna expedition of 1560, the Napochies disappear from the historical record until 1700. The sixteenth-century Napochie towns described by Luna's forces were probably the Audubon Acres and Citico archaeological sites near present-day Chattanooga, Tennessee. These towns were abandoned before the end of the sixteenth century, and two towns were established north of the Tennessee River in Moccasin Bend. A third settlement was established on nearby Williams Island in the Chattanooga area by the early seventeenth century. It is possible that the Napochies moved north to put the Tennessee River between themselves and the Coosa Indians and their Spanish allies. These towns were abandoned by about 1630. We can hypothesize that their inhabitants moved downstream to the Guntersville Reservoir area of the Tennessee River. Seventeenth-century archaeological sites are known in this area (Smith 1987, 1989b; Webb and Wilder 1952). The Napochies reenter history in 1700 when they appear on a town list prepared by the Frenchman Charles Levasseur as the "Napaches" (Knight and Adams 1981:51). They are listed immediately after the Alebamons, a group located near the junction of the Coosa and Tallapoosa rivers, suggesting that they lived in this area. This location is borne out in the Barnwell map of ca. 1722, which appears to list Nabootche (the legend is not clear) opposite Fort Toulouse. The town does not appear on Popple's 1733 map or on French maps of the 1730s, indicating that the town amalgamated with another by this time.

Tuskigee

The Tasqui of de Soto and Pardo and the Tasquiqui of Pardo lived in eastern Tennessee, based on recent efforts to trace the de Soto route (DePratter, Hudson, and Smith 1985). Charles Levasseur's town list of 1700 includes "Tascqui" (Knight and Adams 1981). Swanton notes that a few early eighteenth-century maps, such as the Homann maps and the Seale map, place "Tuskegee" near the headwaters of the Coosa. They are placed on the Coosa River north of the Abihka on the Couvens and Mortier map of the early eighteenth century (Swanton 1922:209). They appear as the "Taskequi" between the Conchatez (Koasati) and the Abieikas (Abihkas) on the Delisle map of 1718. The "Tasquiki" appear opposite Fort Toulouse on the western bank of the Coosa River on the de Crenay map of 1733. They are also in the same location as the "Teskigees" on the Bonar map of 1757 (fig. 17). The Tuskigee appear on the Mitchell map of 1755 as the "Jaskegee" and are located near the junction of the Coosa and Tallapoosa rivers. They do not appear on the Purcell map of 1770.

David Taitt noted in 1772 that the Tuskigee lived near the abandoned French Fort Toulouse. They were "a remnant of northern Indians and speak a different language from the Creeks. They had 25 gun men and one Indian gun merchant" (Mereness 1916:541). If we take the maps at face value, the Tasquiqui gradually migrated south, following largely the same route as the Coosa and Abihkas. However, they continued farther south to the junction of the Coosa and Tallapoosa rivers by the 1730s. Remnants of Taskigi town make up the Poarch Band of Creek Indians living today near Atmore, Alabama (Tony Parades, personal communication).

Quasate (Koasati)

The Koasati of the eighteenth century may have been the same group as the Coste of de Soto and the Costehe of Pardo (Swanton 1922:201). We believe that in 1540 their principal town was at the junction of the Little Tennessee River with the Tennessee River on Bussell Island (DePratter, Hudson, and Smith 1985). They are not mentioned in Bishop Calderón's town list of 1675, but they receive extended notice by Marcos Delgado in 1686, when they are located on the upper Alabama River: "On leaving here there is another place one league distance called Qusate of an unknown nation which came a great distance from the north, fleeing from the English and Chichumeco people which are the greatest conquerors among all the nations of Florida. This village has more than 500 warriors and is on the very bank of the river which goes to Mobila" (Boyd 1937:26).

Thus by the late seventeenth century, they appear on the Lower Coosa or Alabama River headwaters, near the junction of the Coosa and Tallapoosa rivers in central Alabama. This is a considerable move to the south. Thomas Nairne's 1711 map of the Southeast continues to call the Tennessee River the Cussate River, but he located a hundred Cussate men at the headwaters of the Coosa River. Does this show an out-of-date location, or did the group split into two parts in the late seventeenth century? We may never know.

Tuasi

The Tuasi of the de Soto period were believed to have been located in northern Alabama, perhaps at the Polecat Ford site. Bishop Calderón's list of towns mentions the "Tubassi" in 1675 apparently living near the junction of the Coosa and Tallapoosa. Marcos Delgado lists the "Tuave" in this general location in 1686. Eventually the Towassas joined the Alabama-Koasati people near Fort Toulouse.

Ulibahali

Ulibahali of the de Soto period was believed to have been located near the site of present-day Rome, Georgia. Perhaps this was at the Coosa Country Club site at the head of the Coosa River (Smith 1987). There is little mention of these people in later years. However, Daniel Coxe, writing in

1722, places the "Ullibalies" on the Coosa River south of the Coosas and Abihkas on his map. Coxe clearly derives some of his information from the de Soto narratives. It is likely that Ulibahali had simply ceased to exist by the eighteenth century, since it is not known from any other contemporary source.

There is one other possibility: Coxe discusses "the Ullibalies, or as some, the Olibahalies and according to the French the Allibamous" (Coxe 1722: 24), suggesting that the Ulibahali of the sixteenth century were known to the later French and English as the Alabamas. To confuse the issue further, an Alibamu town mentioned in the de Soto narratives appears to have been located in eastern Mississippi (Hudson 1990a). I suspect that these Alabamu moved to the east to become the eighteenth-century Alabama (Smith 1987, 1989b). It is likely that Coxe's equation of Ullibalies with Allibamous is in error, because he relied on second-hand sources and never visited the area.

Remnants of Coosa in Other Drainages

Other groups of the sixteenth-century paramount chiefdom of Coosa appear to have moved elsewhere. Chiaha and Yuchi, located in present-day eastern Tennessee in de Soto and Pardo's day, became important towns among the Lower Creeks on the Chattahoochee River below the fall line near modern Columbus, Georgia. However, these settlements are beyond the scope of the area under study, and we will not consider them further. Many groups seem to have simply disappeared from the historical record. We assume that much of their population died from the effects of European disease and warfare while survivors amalgamated with other towns.

Historical accounts of Coosa of the sixteenth century and Coosa (Upper Creeks) of the eighteenth century have been presented in chapters 3 and 4. What remains is to identify sixteenth-century Coosa archaeologically, as is done in chapter 5. It becomes readily apparent, from historical sketches, that Coosa of the eighteenth century bear little resemblance to those of the sixteenth century, and this transformation will be the subject of chapter 6.

5

Identifying Coosa

The Sixteenth Century

The Spanish expeditions of the sixteenth century left valuable information about the chiefdom of Coosa, yet the problem remained of how to locate Coosa on the ground. De Soto himself was usually lost as he traveled through the Southeast, so reconstructing his route was a difficult problem. Many scholars have attempted to trace the route of Hernando de Soto in the past. The United States De Soto Expedition Commission made the most scholarly effort for the four hundredth anniversary of the expedition (Swanton 1939). The commission, headed by John R. Swanton, took information from three accounts—those of Ranjel, Elvas, and Biedma—and from the history compiled by Garcilaso de la Vega. They used vague mentions of travel direction, distances traveled (only occasionally mentioned), days traveled between towns, and geographic clues such as river crossings, mountains, and so forth. Swanton also drew on information provided by many earlier scholars, along with that provided by contemporary historians and archaeologists. Working with certain assumptions, such as that Indian towns did not move between the sixteenth and eighteenth centuries, the commission proposed a route. Unfortunately, archaeological knowledge was still in its infancy.

The Archaeology of Sixteenth-Century Coosa

While Swanton's commission proposed a route that appeared to fit the known evidence, more recent archaeological research has cast serious doubts on their route (Brain 1985). Of particular interest here is the commission's location of Coosa: "Coca is one of the best established points along De Soto's route. With few exceptions, students have agreed that it was the Upper Creek town of Coosa, one which occupied a prominent place in Creek history and legend and stood on Coosa River between the mouths of Tallasseehatchee and Talladega creeks but nearer the latter, in the present Talladega County, Alabama" (Swanton 1939:206). Archaeological research designed to test this proposition in 1948 proved that this location, called the Childersburg archaeological site, was a purely eighteenth-century occupation and could not have been de Soto's Coosa (DeJarnette and Hansen 1960). With that hypothesis destroyed, and other parts of the commission's route equally in doubt, new research began.

By the 1970s and early 1980s, archaeologists had learned much about southeastern archaeology and the materials the Spanish explorers might have carried. Museum studies in Europe and excavations of Spanish colonial town sites in Florida, South Carolina, and the Caribbean provided much valuable information concerning Spanish ceramics, arms, and armor and Indian trade objects such as beads, bells, axes, and other items. Radiocarbon dating, a technique not available to Swanton and his commission, helped to date more accurately the archaeological remains of native societies of the sixteenth century. De Soto had marched from one Indian society to another in search of wealth and food for his army. Knowing which Indian towns existed at the time of the expedition was a large help in determining where he had been. However, he certainly did not visit all such towns.

Native peoples traded European artifacts over long distances, so the presence of such datable evidence does not ensure the direct presence of Spaniards. Evidence that the Indians passed down (heirloomed) European artifacts over generations is weak. Rather, archaeological and historical evidence suggests that owners of European materials, usually chiefs or other important people in the mid-sixteenth century, were often buried with their wealth. For example, de Soto found European beads and an axe in a mortuary temple at Talimico in present-day South Carolina. The Spaniards believed that these objects came from the Ayllón colony that had attempted to settle the coast in 1526. Thus these materials would have reached mortuary deposits within fourteen years and would have traveled at least a hundred miles from any possible Ayllón landfall.

Evidence from the King site in Georgia suggests that the elite were interred with the European items they had obtained during their lifetimes. And while European artifacts are not direct evidence of the presence of Spaniards, they are sensitive chronological markers. They yield valuable clues as to which towns the Indians occupied in the mid-sixteenth century. We can therefore determine which towns the Spanish explorers could have visited.

Several attempts to reconstruct portions of de Soto's route failed because no one started at the beginning and followed de Soto across the entire Southeast. Finally, in the late 1970s, several scholars led by Charles Hudson began a concerted effort. Their goal was to trace de Soto's entire route from his landing in Florida to the expedition's escape down the Mississippi River.

While the new archaeological knowledge uncovered by this project was invaluable, the real breakthrough came with the location of a little-known account of the later expedition of Juan Pardo. Chester DePratter, then one of Hudson's graduate students, relocated a long account by the scribe of the Pardo expedition, Juan de la Bandera. This account was much more detailed than any record of the de Soto expedition. However, since Pardo had visited many of the same towns as de Soto, it became the key to locating the routes of both expeditions (DePratter, Hudson, and Smith 1983; Hudson 1990a, 1990b, 1997; Hudson et al. 1985).

Hudson, Smith, and DePratter studied the information from the reconstructed Pardo expedition, the earlier de Soto and Luna expeditions, and the new archaeological evidence, including those Indian towns that had yielded sixteenth-century Spanish trade goods. Using this information, they identified the location of sixteenth-century Coosa as the Little Egypt archaeological site on the Coosawattee River in northwestern Georgia. They also identified a number of other likely archaeological sites visited by the various expeditions (DePratter, Hudson, and Smith 1985; Hudson et al. 1985; Smith 1987).

Later research on the expedition of a detachment of forces from the Tristán de Luna expedition shed additional light on Coosa (Hudson et al. 1989). Eight towns of Coosa were mentioned in the Davila Padilla account. This number closely matches the six villages and three smaller archaeological sites currently known from the Coosawattee Valley. The Domingo de la Anunciación account mentions a mountain range to the north and indicates that two small rivers unite within the town—again consistent with the setting of the Little Egypt site. The account of the expedition to the Napochies fits well with the known distribution of archaeological sites. The description of the river of the Napochies could fit only the Tennessee River. Also, there are sixteenth-century archaeological sites in precisely the position called for in the Luna narratives near present-day Chattanooga, Tennessee (Smith 1987).

While the core of the chiefdom of Coosa was the Coosawattee River area, by de Soto's day Coosa held sway over people from central Alabama to northern Tennessee. Evidence from the Sauz detachment of the Luna expedition suggests some collapse, but an account from the Pardo expedition again suggests that Coosa was a stable place with many allies.

The archaeological picture of mid-sixteenth-century Coosa has been the subject of research by David Hally, Marvin Smith, and James Langford (1990). They found several site clusters from that period. These were located primarily where major streams cross the Cartersville Fault separating the Piedmont or Blue Ridge Province from the Ridge and Valley (fig. 18). The importance of this ecotone location was discussed in relation to the Coosawattee Valley sites. The same points hold true for other similar locations up and down the valley. Figure 18 presents the known distribution of sixteenth-century archaeological sites in the region. According to the Spaniards, all of these towns were under the influence of Coosa. The nature of this influence, however, is hard to define.

There are many clusters of five to eight archaeological sites. In several cases, these clusters are apparently the provinces mentioned in the Spanish narratives. Thus, the sites clustered near Chattanooga are likely the Napochie towns of the Luna accounts. The cluster near Cartersville corresponds to the Itaba of the de Soto accounts. The cluster near present-day Rome, Georgia, would include Ulibahali, Apica, and unnamed village(s) of de Soto and Luna. A cluster of sites on the Little Tennessee

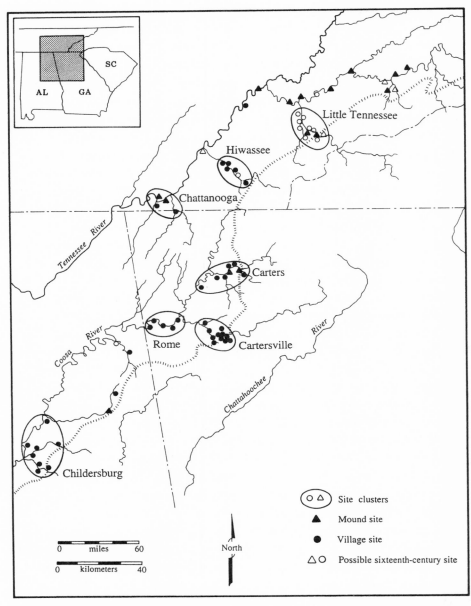

18. Archaeological sites of the Coosa Paramount Chiefdom. Map by Julie Barnes Smith.

drainage includes de Soto's Coste and Tali and Pardo's Satapo and Chalahume. The cluster on the Hiwassee River probably includes de Soto's
Tasqui and perhaps Pardo's Tasquiqui. The cluster of towns in the Childersburg, Alabama, area would be the province of Talisi. Finally, towns
on and around Zimmerman's Island probably represent Chiaha.

There are five to thirteen known archaeological sites in each of the
seven identified clusters. The size of each town cluster is approximately
20 km in diameter—small enough that a provincial chief could have visited any town in his realm in a single day. Large uninhabited zones between these units of multiple towns served as wild game reservoirs and
political buffers. Most of the archaeological sites appear to be villages of
about 2.8 ha on average (ranging from 1 to 5.6 ha). The rare sites smaller
than 1 ha are probably special-purpose sites or farmsteads. The Childersburg cluster is problematical. The site sizes are suspiciously large,
ranging from 1.5 to 8 ha, and may be overestimated. Thus, this cluster is
not considered in the figures presented.

Hally, Smith, and Langford (1990:table 9.1) have used formulas developed to estimate the number of inhabitants of roofed areas (that is, household size) as well as village size and the number of villages. They estimate
a population between 2,847 and 5,401 for the Coosawattee cluster—the
central Coosa area. The resulting figures depend on which estimate of
population per floor area is used (Cook 1972; Naroll 1962). Naroll suggests an estimate of one person per 10 square meters of floor area. Cook
suggests an estimate nearly twice as high. Hally and his colleagues estimate that the average town had between 350 and 652 individuals. By
using these figures when site size is unknown, and excluding some poorly
known sites that may be slightly earlier, we arrive at a rough population
estimate of between 18,000 and 33,500 people for the entire paramount
chiefdom. These figures are probably low, since only winter house size
was measured. Including the small summer houses would probably raise
the estimate by a third, resulting in approximately 24,000 to 45,000
people in the paramount chiefdom from the Childersburg cluster to Zimmerman's Island. A few towns are probably missing, but not all towns
may have been occupied at the same time. It is unlikely that the Paramount Chiefdom of Coosa had a population greater than 50,000.

Major excavations at the Little Egypt site (Hally 1979, 1980, 1983) and
the King site in the Rome cluster (Blakely 1988; Hally 1988, 1994), and

David J. Hally's unpublished work at the Leake site in the Cartersville cluster, have yielded much data on Coosa at the time of the Spanish entradas. Administrative centers usually had mounds while villages did not.

The King site (plate 3a), a medium-size village, is the best known of any of the sites (Hally 1988, 1994; Hally and Kelly 1998). Here the site area is roughly square in plan (480 by 460 ft), and the village was fortified by a ditch and palisade. Two rows of domestic winter houses with adjacent summer houses encircle an open courtyard or plaza. This plaza contains a large public building measuring 50 feet on a side, a smaller special-purpose structure, and some large posts. These posts may have been used for displaying the town emblem, scalps of enemies, torturing captives, or playing games (based on later historical accounts of similar poles).

Winter domestic houses are square to slightly rectangular in floor plan; they are semi-subterranean (the floors were depressed a foot or two into the earth) and measure roughly 25 feet on a side (the range is 18 to 32 ft). They are plastered with clay daub and have interior room dividers and a central hearth. The winter houses were entered via narrow entry passages, probably cut through earthen embanked walls. By building in a pit and banking the earth up against the walls, the builders were able to make well-insulated houses.

The much simpler summer houses were constructed on the ground surface with a few posts. They are recognized in the archaeological record by rectangular post patterns, often with numerous burial pits in the floor. Storage pits or refuse pits were not in common use; apparently storage of food was aboveground in granaries, as described by the Spaniards.

Sixteenth-century pottery of the Coosawattee River drainage of Georgia belongs to the Barnett phase (Hally 1979, 1980). The Barnett phase is characterized by ceramics from two diverse style traditions: Lamar from central Georgia and Dallas from eastern Tennessee. Lamar ceramics are tempered with grit, usually crushed quartz or coarse sand. Common forms include incised constricted (*cazuela*) bowls and complicated stamped storage jars with folded rims. The Dallas tradition of shell-tempered ceramics includes small jars with broad, flat handles and incised decoration, open bowls, and occasionally short-necked water bottle forms. Plate forms, with incised rims, are also known, and they may be shell- or grit-tempered.

Fancy ceramics are rare on Barnett phase sites. However, occasional modeled frog effigy jars of the Dallas tradition (but sometimes tempered with grit) show some artistic endeavor. The Barnett phase ceramics show an interesting blend of attributes from the north and the south, often on the same vessel. Perhaps the diversity of Barnett phase pottery reflects the cosmopolitan nature of the paramount chiefdom.

David Hally's extensive work at the Little Egypt site has produced much information about subsistence remains of the sixteenth-century Coosa. Roth (1980) has reported on the food bone from Little Egypt. Fish, especially drum, make up to 25 percent of the remains from some areas of the site, while deer provide 39–84 percent of the identified bones. The Coosa also hunted black bear, but the types of bones found suggest that they were not a major food source. Other mammals hunted include raccoon, squirrel, opossum, and beaver. Wild turkey was a common food source, while passenger pigeon was rarely eaten. Shellfish were present but added little to the diet.

Hally (1981) reports plant remains from the Little Egypt site. Cultivated plants include corn, beans, and squash, the common cultigens for all of eastern North America. Other species utilized include persimmon, honey locust, pokeweed, grape, bear's foot, gourd, plum, maypop, and knotweed. These species are found on most late prehistoric archaeological sites in eastern North America. Nuts, another important part of the diet, included hickory, acorn, black walnut, and butternut.

Subsistence remains from the Toqua site in Tennessee can be compared to those from Little Egypt. Not surprisingly, deer make up the largest component of the animal remains, followed by bear and turkey. Other species utilized include elk, bison, small mammals, waterfowl, passenger pigeon, turtles, fish, and a few mollusks (Bogan 1987:1108). Plant food remains include the domesticates maize, beans, squash, gourd, sumpweed, and sunflower. Wild species include acorn, hickory nut, walnut, butternut, grape, maypop, smartweed, morning glory, composite, persimmon, chenopod, wild bean, and bearsfoot. Also used were pokeweed, ragweed, honey locust, bedstraw, wild cherry, sumac, hawthorn, crab apple, black locust, and wild grass (Shea, Polhemus, and Chapman 1987: 1202–3).

Burial treatment and accompanying grave goods at sixteenth-century sites in northern Georgia are unspectacular in comparison to the earlier

Savannah-Wilbanks examples from the Etowah site, Bell Field Mound graves, or earlier Dallas burials from the eastern Tennessee area. Log tombs or stone box graves were no longer constructed, indicating much less effort in the burial ritual. If one assumes that mound interments represented the social elites, grave goods are not impressive. Burials recovered from Mound A at the Little Egypt site generally have the same grave goods as those from the village area at Little Egypt or from the nonmound King site.

Some artifacts appear to have been sixteenth-century markers of high status. These include shell bowls found at Little Egypt and in the burial with the highest-quality accompaniments at the King site. The preeminent burial at the King site yielded arrowhead-shaped copper ornaments. Other high-status artifacts are massive stone axe blades from Little Egypt and spatulate (spade-shaped) stone axe blades from the King and Leake sites (see fig. 19a).

European artifacts are often found in grave contexts together with these native artifact types, which suggests that they were hoarded by the elite of the society (M. Smith 1987). Swords apparently held special fascination. Moorehead (1932) found the remains of a sword and a large stone axe blade in a burial at the Little Egypt site. The King site sword (plate 3a) came from a grave that also contained a spatulate axe, three large flint knives, a stone pipe, and a cache of arrowheads (probably signifying a bundle of arrows) (Little 1985). Sword fragments are also known from Poarch Farm, Johnstone Farm, and Etowah in northern Georgia (Smith 1992:100–101).

Other grave goods found in Little Egypt mound contexts and village contexts in northern Georgia include stone arrowheads and shell gorgets engraved with a rattlesnake motif (fig. 20). Shell beads, shell earpins, bipointed flint knives (a shorter form of the long chert "swords" found in earlier contexts at Etowah; see fig. 19b), ceramic pipes, and pottery vessels were also found. Pottery vessels found in Barnett phase burial contexts do not appear to be specialized forms but rather common utility vessels. Plain or engraved shell masks, turtle shell leg rattles, and chunky stones are also found in village burial contexts.

How did Coosa, originally just another small chiefdom, expand its influence to become a paramount chiefdom, and when was the consolidation of the Ridge and Valley area accomplished? It is easier to answer

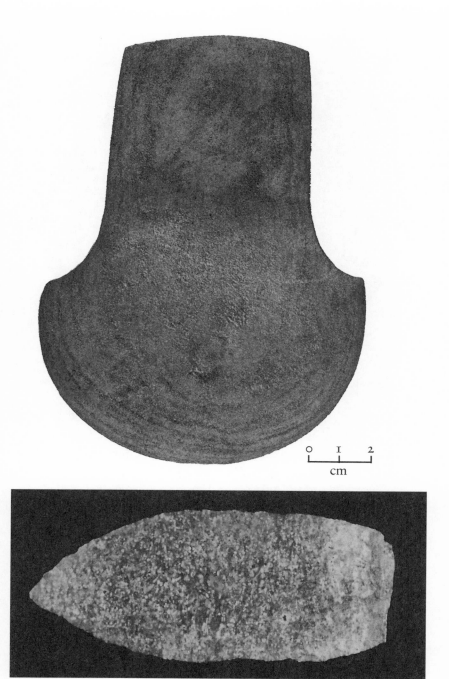

o   I   2

cm

19. Aboriginal status markers, King site. *A*, spatulate axe; *B*, flaked knife. Photos courtesy Gordon L. Hight.

O   I   2
cm

20. Rattlesnake gorget, King site. Photo courtesy Gordon L. Hight.

"when" before "how. Clearly Coosa could not have held sway in the region while Etowah was at its height. It is possible that Etowah had already consolidated political power in the region during the thirteenth and early fourteenth centuries. There is evidence that some ceramic motifs were in common use throughout the area, and engraved shell gorgets from eastern Tennessee share motifs with those from the Etowah site. (Note that the Etowah complicated stamped diamond motif is actually widespread far beyond the Ridge and Valley.) Some copper ornaments, such as the bilobed arrow form, also occur in both areas.

The collapse of Etowah around the mid-fourteenth century probably produced a sort of power vacuum for some time. Eventually Coosa filled this vacuum. Given the argument that the shift in mound centers in the Coosawattee Valley reflects an inherent political instability of the region, it is unlikely that the chiefdom of Coosa existed before the founding of the Little Egypt mound site, sometime around A.D. 1400. If this argument is valid, the Coosa chiefdom arose sometime around 1400 and had evolved into the paramount chiefdom visited by the Spaniards in less than a century and a half. That it could grow from a couple of villages on the Coosawattee River at about A.D. 1400 to consolidate power over large portions of Tennessee, Georgia, and Alabama only 140 years later is truly amazing.

How did the chiefdom of Coosa on the Coosawattee River become the paramount chiefdom of Coosa controlling an area 400 kilometers long? This question is much harder to answer. The number of villages on the Coosawattee increased between the Little Egypt phase of the fifteenth century and the Barnett phase of the sixteenth century. We might suggest on logical grounds that population increases led to increasing power. The emphasis on militarism seen by the Spaniards in sixteenth-century chiefdoms, and observable archaeologically in much of the complex iconography from prehistoric mound centers, suggests that warfare was endemic. Perhaps population growth in the Coosawattee Valley simply allowed the chief of Coosa to overrun his nearest neighbor, perhaps the village clusters at Cartersville or Rome. As one enemy was conquered and tributary status established, the resulting polity, now roughly twice the size of the original Coosa (or any other cluster), would have had little trouble conquering the next neighbor, and so on down the line. It is likely that many groups simply submitted to Coosa's authority as the polity snowballed in size. Paying tribute in goods or furnishing warriors was far simpler than fighting a war against a foe many times the size of one's own polity. But what caused the initial population growth in the Coosawattee Valley? Was it natural increase, or the result of in-migration, or even a combination of factors? Perhaps the growing power of this valley attracted people from the disintegrating Etowah chiefdom. Of course, all of this discussion is primarily speculative, but something like this must have happened during the fifteenth and early sixteenth centuries if the Spanish accounts of Coosa are to be believed.

Another possiblity is that Coosa exercised little real power over its neighbors. Instead of a conquest paramount chiefdom, the political entity of Coosa visited by the Spaniards may have been little more than a mutual nonaggression pact among groups in the Ridge and Valley Province. It is always better to have allies when warfare is rampant than to stand alone. Coosa may have achieved some power simply because it was near the center of the physiographic region whose inhabitants shared a common adaptation.

The Spanish accounts are unfortunately not clear on the nature of the alliance. Tribute is mentioned and towns are said "to be subject to Coosa," but exactly what these terms mean is not known. In all probability, the chief of Coosa did not have absolute power over his subject chiefs. Each constituent chiefdom probably functioned as a separate entity in most day-to-day affairs. They clearly cooperated in military ventures and paid Coosa some form of tribute. Little is known of the nature of this tribute, but the Napochies were forced to contribute game, fruits, and nuts to Coosa after they were resubjugated by combined Coosa-Luna forces in 1560. Tribute may also have taken the form of exotic trade goods and storable agricultural surplus.

Chiefs often consolidated power, placing their relatives in charge of other towns. Marriage alliances often cemented political alliances (Anderson 1994). Unfortunately, there is no documentary evidence of such alliances between groups in the Coosa paramount chiefdom. The Spaniards probably did not understand the matrilineal kinship structure of the southeastern Indians, and they did not record much information useful to modern anthropologists.

Another theory suggests that trade in elite luxury items may have been used to consolidate power (Spencer 1987:376). Etowah likely controlled sources of copper in the fourteenth century, but by the sixteenth century it was not a common luxury good. Indeed, fifteenth- and sixteenth-century archaeological sites are known for their impoverished nature compared to the sites of the thirteenth and fourteenth centuries. Grave goods from the sixteenth century usually consist of everyday cooking pots, stone tools, and some shell beads or gorgets (pendants). About the only artifacts that appear to reflect high social status are the bipointed flint knives and spatulate celts discussed earlier. European metal items and glass beads quickly became status symbols during the sixteenth century. It is hard to imagine a chief controlling access to stone tools, since raw materials and the simple technology necessary for production were available to all. Unless more perishable luxury goods were in use, such as feather work or special textiles, it is hard to attribute the rise of Coosa to the control of elite luxury goods. While there is evidence that elites controlled the trade in European items (Smith 1987), it was clearly a post-founding phenomenon because Coosa was already a paramount chiefdom when the Spaniards arrived.

Coosa and Other Sixteenth-Century Chiefdoms in the Southeast

Coosa was certainly not the only chiefdom in the Southeast during de Soto's day, but it may well have been the largest in territory. The nearest paramount chiefdoms in the area were Cofitachequi, which controlled much of the Piedmont of North and South Carolina (DePratter 1994); Ocute, which controlled the Oconee River drainage in the Georgia Piedmont (see Williams 1994); and Tascaluca, which controlled the upper Alabama River drainage in central Alabama (fig. 8). Only Cofitachequi may have rivaled Coosa in territory, although the evidence for its size is not as clear as that for Coosa. Charles Hudson has suggested that Cofitachequi's power may have extended from the coast at Port Royal Sound all the way north into the Asheville, North Carolina, area (1990b).

It is interesting to note that Coosa's fame was known by the residents of Patofa, a town on the upper Oconee River in the eastern Georgia Piedmont that was allied with Ocute. The natives of Patofa told de Soto "towards the northwest there was a province called Coca, a plentiful country having very large towns. The Cacique [chief] told the Governor that if he desired to go thither he would give him a guide and Indians to carry burdens" (Elvas 1968:58). The location of Patofa is nearly 100 miles (161 km) to the southeast of Coosa's capital.

Other chiefdoms visited by de Soto in Arkansas had large towns with large populations, but their territory was small compared to that of Coosa. As far as we know from archaeology and the fragments of description left by Spanish explorers, Coosa was unique in the sixteenth century. It is the only large paramount chiefdom that had consolidated political power over several other chiefdoms in a large region. For its widespread influence and power, it may be comparable to prehistoric chiefdoms centered on the Etowah site in Georgia, the Moundville site in Alabama, or the Cahokia site in Illinois.

6

The Lost Years

Following the Spanish exploration of the mid-sixteenth century, Coosa fades from the light of historical documentation. Coosa is not mentioned in the 1675 letter of Spanish Bishop Calderón, which enumerates many of the known Indian towns of the interior at the time (Wenhold 1936).

Likewise it is not mentioned by Marcos Delgado, a Spaniard sent to check on rumors of Frenchmen penetrating the Southeast in 1686 (Boyd 1937). Delgado reached at least the area of the lower Tallapoosa Valley in Alabama, but he does not mention Coosa or Abihka farther north.

The French brought the first real mention of the Coosa towns back to written history. In 1700, Charles Levasseur compiled a list of Indian towns on the Alabama, Coosa, and Tallapoosa rivers (Knight and Adams 1981). It includes Apicales (Abihka), Talisi, Tascqui, Ouacoussa, and Napaches (Napochies). (Knight and Adams interpret Tascqui as Tuskegee of the eighteenth century, but it could also be identified with the Tasqui of the de Soto narratives. They cautiously suggest that Ouacoussa may be Coosa.) Thus from 1568 until 1700 there is virtually no historical documentation for any town of the Coosa paramount chiefdom. Tracing the story of these people becomes an archaeological problem once again.

The period from 1568 until about 1700 was a time of cultural and population collapse for the Coosa people (Smith 1987). Anthropologists and historians have long known that the introduction of Old World diseases into native American populations had a devastating effect. Diseases that had evolved in the Old World struck much harder in the New World because the natives had not developed any natural resistance or immunity over centuries of adaptation as Old World populations had (Dobyns 1983; Ramenofsky 1987). What were merely childhood diseases in the Old World, such as measles, became destructive plagues in the New World. Also, the horrible plagues of the Old World, such as bubonic plague, were equally destructive to Native Americans. Evidence from the Coosa area suggests that local people were hard hit by epidemics throughout the late sixteenth and seventeenth centuries. Multiple burials are possible archaeological evidence of such epidemics. Graves of more than one individual interred together (fig. 21) are found on sixteenth- and seventeenth-century sites in the study area (Smith 1987).

The epidemics, perhaps combined with other factors, started a series of population movements. By the end of the sixteenth century, northern Georgia was abandoned and the Coosa people moved downstream into present-day Alabama. Subsequently, they migrated farther south at intervals of about thirty years. It is hard to determine whether these migrations reflect a flight from epidemics of European disease or were prompted by a changing balance of power, altered trading relations, or other causes. These migrations will be documented in greater detail later in this chapter.

With a great loss of population, the hierarchical chiefdom organization of the Coosa people crumbled (Smith 1987). There were simply not enough people left to produce the food and to make up the labor surpluses needed to support an elite stratum of society. Construction of monumental public works, a characteristic of many chiefdoms around the world (Peebles and Kus 1977), ceased. Thus platform mounds were no longer built in the Coosa area by the early seventeenth century. Hierarchies of sites, seen in size of community and number of mounds, ceased to exist. Whereas there had been multi-mound centers, single-mound secondary administrative centers, large villages, smaller villages, and in some cases hamlets and farmsteads, now only villages, hamlets, and

21. Multiple burial, King site. Photo courtesy Gordon L. Hight.

farmsteads remained. There was a change from compact towns to more dispersed settlement over the course of the seventeenth century. Special elite dwelling and burial areas disappeared, and fancy elite sumptuary goods were rarely manufactured by the mid-seventeenth century.

Before proceeding to describe the seventeenth-century movements of the Coosa people, we must digress and discuss methods of dating the sites in the study. Unfortunately, radiocarbon dating is not accurate enough to be of use for this recent period. We are interested in seeing settlement changes over short periods, and the large statistical range of probability for radiocarbon dates renders them insufficiently precise for our purposes. Attempts to use radiocarbon dating in the northwest Georgia area for sites of the sixteenth century have been largely futile. For example, four radiocarbon dates for the King site, known to have had a short occupation based on house rebuildings and other evidence, are A.D. 1410, 1670, 1830, and "modern" (Hally 1975:51; these are uncorrected dates). In this instance we may be dealing with some contamination, perhaps caused by industrial fertilizers or some other factor. The radiocarbon calibration curve is very erratic over the interval of interest, and that may be the main reason for the apparent anomaly (V. J. Knight, personal communication). Other archaeological dating techniques, such as thermoluminescence or paleomagnetism, likewise have not been successfully applied in the area.

With traditional techniques failing to provide accurate dates, a method has been developed of dating aboriginal sites by cross-dating European trade or gift items found in those sites (Smith 1987). Certain styles of artifacts can be dated by reference to artifacts from documented Spanish colonial town sites or European museum collections. Thus experts on arms and armor have dated a sword from the King site to the early sixteenth century (Little 1985). A style of glass bead, called a Nueva Cádiz bead after a Spanish colonial town site on an island off the coast of Venezuela, can be dated ca. 1519–50 on historical and archaeological grounds (Smith and Good 1982). Other glass-bead styles can be dated from their contexts at Spanish colonial towns such as St. Augustine or Santa Elena on the Atlantic coast of North America and excavated Spanish missions of the seventeenth century that are historically documented (Deagan 1987; DePratter and Smith 1980; Smith 1983). Styles of bells, prized by the Indians, also underwent changes (I. Brown 1979). Other items include iron chisels, known to have been traded by Juan Pardo (but also found later) and perhaps included in the "iron implements" traded by Hernando de Soto. There are also iron axes, horseshoes, a crossbow bolt tip, an engraved copper plaque, chain mail (plate 2), and other miscellaneous items. Examining not only the type of European artifacts present but also the proportion of European and aboriginal artifacts in graves, researchers have been able to establish a chronology of sites. Most excavated sites can be dated to within roughly a third of a century.

Aboriginal pottery, which underwent steady stylistic change, can be compared. Thus many sites that have not been excavated enough to produce European artifacts—which are usually limited to grave furniture in the early sites—can be dated by comparison of pottery types with those from excavated sites that have produced datable European artifacts. Given this close dating capability, changes in population and settlement pattern can be detected.

Coosa Migrates Southward

The location of the sixteenth-century towns of the Coosa chiefdom was described in chapter 5. However, the inhabitants moved soon thereafter, perhaps because of the epidemics. The evidence is particularly clear in sites along the Coosa drainage of northern Georgia and will form the focus for discussion. The situation in eastern Tennessee is not as clear and detailed movements are not documented, although some suggestions have been made (Smith 1989b).

Currently, some eighteen villages are known from northwestern Georgia dating to the sixteenth century (Hally, Smith, and Langford 1990). These sites comprise three large clusters: the Carters cluster, the Cartersville cluster, and the Rome cluster (see fig. 18). There are twenty-four more sites in Tennessee and perhaps a few in the northeastern corner of Alabama. Farther south, near present-day Childersburg, Alabama, there is a cluster of eight Kymulga phase sites. These may represent the Talisi Province mentioned in the de Soto narratives. The north Georgia towns were abandoned before the end of the sixteenth century.

A distinctive assemblage of European artifacts, in which new styles of glass beads appear, has been defined for the late sixteenth century (Smith 1987). It is based on comparisons with other dated sites in North

America. Sites containing this artifact assemblage are unknown in north-western Georgia (there is one possible, poorly documented exception on the state line) but have been found just to the west, at the Polecat Ford site in Alabama (1Ce308) (Little and Curren 1981) (fig. 22). The implication is that all of northwestern Georgia was abandoned before the end of the sixteenth century, and the Coosa people moved down the Coosa drainage into present-day Alabama. Itaba, Ulibahali, Apica, and Piachi and their unnamed related towns of the Carters, Cartersville, and Rome site clusters left northwest Georgia. The migrants may have facilitated movement downstream by simply floating their possessions down the river in dugout canoes or rafts. The current archaeological evidence indicates that depopulation was so massive that eighteen towns were reduced to only one, but it is suspected that some smaller, late sixteenth-century village sites will eventually be located, perhaps up small tributaries of the Coosa River. It is possible, of course, that the decimation of the population really was as pronounced as the absence of late sixteenth-century villages indicates.

By approximately 1585, the Polecat Ford site was apparently abandoned, the inhabitants moving down Terrapin Creek to establish a new site at its junction with the Coosa River (Holstein et al. 1990; Smith 1987). The Terrapin Creek site (1Ce309) (fig. 23) was relatively small, measuring less than two hectares in extent (Holstein et al. 1990). The aboriginal pottery from this site shows the beginnings of a departure from the combination of shell-tempered and grit-tempered Lamar types of the Barnett phase. There is a shift to a preponderance of shell-tempered ceramics, which characterize seventeenth-century sites in the region. Lamar types are still present at Terrapin Creek, but they form a distinct minority (Holstein et al. 1990:table 36). The Terrapin Creek site shows a few glass bead styles that are typical of the sixteenth century but the majority of the beads are identical to those from subsequent early seventeenth-century sites. Terrapin Creek also produced shell beads that are absent from nearby early seventeenth-century sites. For these reasons, Terrapin Creek is assigned an approximate date range of ca. 1585–1600.

By the beginning of the seventeenth century, the archaeological picture comes into better focus. There is a distinct cluster of early seventeenth-century sites in and around the hydroelectric reservoir Lake Weiss on the Coosa River near the Alabama-Georgia border (see fig. 23) (DeJarnette,

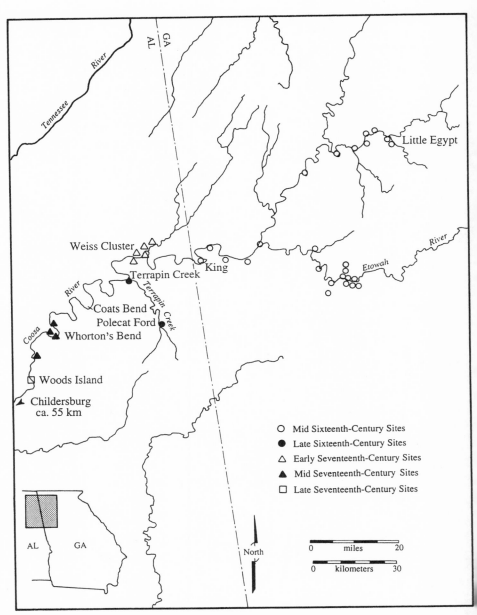

Little Egypt

Weiss Cluster

King

Terrapin Creek

Coats Bend
Polecat Ford
Whorton's Bend

Woods Island

Childersburg
ca. 55 km

Tennessee River

Coosa River

Terrapin Creek

Etowah River

○ Mid Sixteenth-Century Sites
● Late Sixteenth-Century Sites
△ Early Seventeenth-Century Sites
▲ Mid Seventeenth-Century Sites
□ Late Seventeenth-Century Sites

AL GA

North

0   miles   20
0   kilometers   30

22. Archaeological sites of the Coosa drainage. Map by Julie Barnes Smith.

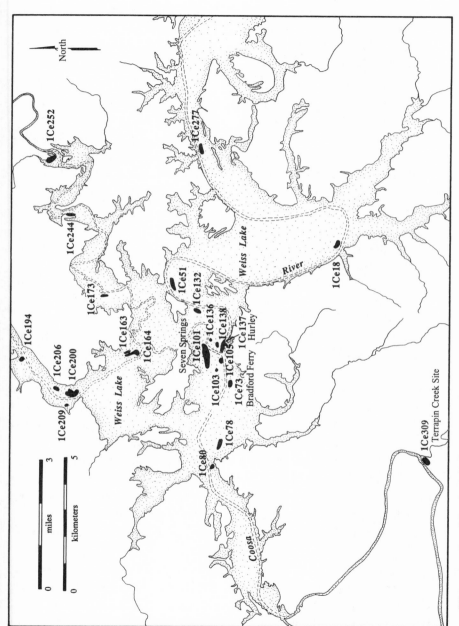

23. Weiss area sites. Map by Julie Barnes Smith.

Kurjack, and Keel 1973; Holstein, Hill, and Little 1997; Smith 1987, 1989a). These sites include the excavated Bradford Ferry and Seven Springs villages, the Gilmore Springs small hamlet or farmstead (De-Jarnette et al. 1973; Smith 1987, 1989a), and the Hurley site village (Holstein, Hill, and Little 1997; Holstein et al. 1992).

The aboriginal pottery indicates that there are several other sites in the cluster. Site Ce252, represented by surface collections only, appears to have been a village. Thirteen other sites appear to be small hamlets or farmsteads (Smith 1989a). It could be suggested that the four villages in the area were the political centers of the now-defunct Coosa chiefdom (Coosawattee cluster), Itaba (Cartersville cluster), and Ulibahali-Apica (Rome cluster). Perhaps the fourth site represents the Terrapin Creek people.

Under the pressure of European disease epidemics, each sixteenth-century cluster may have amalgamated into one large site with some accompanying farmsteads. Together these sites form a cluster approximately 13 km in maximum extent. The Seven Springs site, the largest known from the cluster, is also centrally located and is situated at the junction of the Coosa River with the Little River/Chatooga River system. The Bradford Ferry village, 1Ce73, is located across the Coosa River from Seven Springs, and the Hurley site, 1Ce137, is located across the Chatooga River from Seven Springs. Clearly, these communities took advantage of this strategic junction of rivers.

The choice of this location for settlement shows a major departure from the earlier location of sixteenth-century settlements along the Cartersville Fault. Reasons for the abandonment of this valuable ecotone location are not known, although a beginning reliance on European cutting tools may have lessened the need to obtain suitable stone from the east for ground stone tools. Because the river flows away from the Cartersville Fault area, people moving their belongings downstream via canoe or raft may explain the abandonment of the Cartersville Fault ecotone.

On the other hand, the Weiss Reservoir cluster is in an analogous ecotonal location. It is near the junction of the Lookout Mountain system with the Ridge and Valley Province, so both upland and river-bottom resources were available near the new location. It is suspected that the

Little River drainage system provided good alluvial soil derived from the uplands.

Although large-scale excavations were conducted at Seven Springs and Bradford Ferry, little is known about the daily lives of these people. No house patterns have been discovered; the sites produced only random postholes, burials, and pit features. A wall trench–type structure has been reported from the nearby Hurley site (Holstein, Hill, and Little 1997), but it would be unique at this time level on the Coosa River. Earlier and later sites had houses constructed of single posts. Perhaps the Hurley house is an earlier emergent Mississippian construction. There were no earthworks or fortifications in evidence at the sites, although such features were not specifically sought during excavation. Since these sites were excavated before the development of flotation techniques, virtually no subsistence data were recovered, making it impossible to discuss plant and animal utilization. We can note that peaches, introduced by Europeans, were already common on Indian sites on the Oconee River in Georgia far to the east. These sites are upstream from Spanish missions established on the Georgia coast in the 1560s, so the Indians had easier access to new crops.

The use of refuse-filled pits is noteworthy. These pits are virtually absent from earlier Barnett-phase sites of the sixteenth century, and their presence clearly signals a change in activities. Ward has suggested that storage pits on eighteenth-century sites resulted from increased hunting and consequent winter absenteeism from the towns, which created the need to hide food in underground cache pits (Ward 1985:99). Perhaps these seventeenth-century pits also signal a change in subsistence orientation toward hunting, with a relative decline in agriculture.

Aboriginal ceramics from the Weiss Reservoir sites show a marked change from the earlier sixteenth-century Barnett phase ceramics of northern Georgia. By the early seventeenth century, grit tempering fell virtually out of use. Plain shell-tempered pots or incised shell-tempered bowls and jars appear. The previously popular complicated stamped surface finish almost completely disappeared, although there is a trace of it at Seven Springs. Nevertheless, there is some continuity of incised motifs from the Barnett phase sites to the Weiss sites, although they appear in somewhat different proportions. This continuity suggests that the same

people are involved (Smith 1989a). Holstein and his associates have proposed the term "Weiss phase" for this assemblage (Holstein et al. 1990).

Burial data indicate that—in stark contrast to the sixteenth-century
situation—virtually everyone had access to European goods by the early
seventeenth century. At the sixteenth-century King site, only 2.4 percent
of the 212 burials contained European goods, but at the early seventeenth-century Bradford Ferry site, 66 percent of the 47 burials contained
European artifacts, some containing many European beads, bells, brass
ornaments, or iron tools (plate 4).

The most lavishly accompanied burials were those of children, but
there was no recognizable spatial segregation of any burials that could be
considered an "elite" stratum of society. This situation can be contrasted
with sixteenth-century mound burial of the chief's lineage, strongly argu-
ing for the loss of political hierarchy or ranking (Smith 1987). Assuming
that European disease epidemics caused a decline in population, children
would have become more important to group survival and their loss
would be mourned more than in the late prehistoric period. Relatives
expressed their bereavement by lavishing child burials with grave goods.

The relative abundance of European items is noteworthy, particularly
at a time when Europeans were absent from the interior Southeast. Apparently aboriginal trade networks connected natives in the interior with
Europeans in missionized areas of Florida and the Georgia coast. Waselkov (1989) has suggested that the deerskin trade may have begun at this
early date, although there is almost no documentary evidence for such
trade until the 1640s. In this case, archaeological evidence clearly sup-
plants that from historical sources. Burials at the Weiss Lake sites contain
numerous glass beads, including easily datable chevron beads and eye
beads, numerous brass discs, and brass arm bands. These burials also
contain Clarksdale and Flushloop bells of sheet copper or brass, brass
tinkling cones, and occasional iron celts or eyed axes of the more modern
European form.

Aboriginally made grave goods include pottery vessels, projectile
points, pipes, and red ochre. Goods common in the mid-sixteenth century, such as shell gorgets, shell beads, and stone axe blades, are absent,
replaced by their European counterparts. Although stone axe blades are
not present, ground stone technology did not disappear. Pipes were still

made of ground stone. Flint knapping was also commonly employed for lanceolate or triangular arrow points, much as in the time prior to European contact.

In addition to the Lake Weiss cluster, a smaller group of three sites is located 23 km downstream at Coats Bend of the Coosa River (Harry Holstein, personal communication) (see fig. 22). These sites are known only from small surface collections, but they appear to date to the late sixteenth or early seventeenth century based on the aboriginal ceramics. At least one glass bead had been found on the surface, assuring the historic period placement. It is possible that these sites represent a downstream movement of the Weiss site residents around 1630, but the possibility that the Coats Bend sites are contemporary with the Weiss sites cannot be discounted with the available data. They might even represent some of the missing late sixteenth-century populations in the area.

There are only three Coats Bend sites, and they are rather small (0.9, 0.6, and 1.3 ha). They experienced multiple occupations, so their exact size in the seventeenth century is not known. Clearly, there is no major occupation in this area, but these sites need further investigation to complete our understanding of the population movements.

Gadsden Concentration (Mid-Seventeenth Century)

We are certain the Weiss cluster of sites was abandoned by the 1630s. The people moved downstream again, to Whorton's Bend of the Coosa River, near present-day Gadsden, Alabama (fig. 24). The Coosa River near Gadsden is part of Neely Henry Reservoir. The University of Alabama investigated the archaeological sites there during reservoir construction in the 1960s (Anonymous 1964, 1965; Smith 1989a). Archaeological research in Etowah County dates back to 1948, when a sand-mining operation disturbed burials. The owner of the mine contacted archaeologists David DeJarnette and Steve Wimberly at the University of Alabama, and they undertook salvage excavations at the Milner Village site (Smith et al. 1993). Later reservoir salvage work located several additional sites in the immediate vicinity. Investigations by interested amateur archaeologists resulted in much additional data following reservoir construction as sites were disturbed by construction and later shoreline erosion (Battles

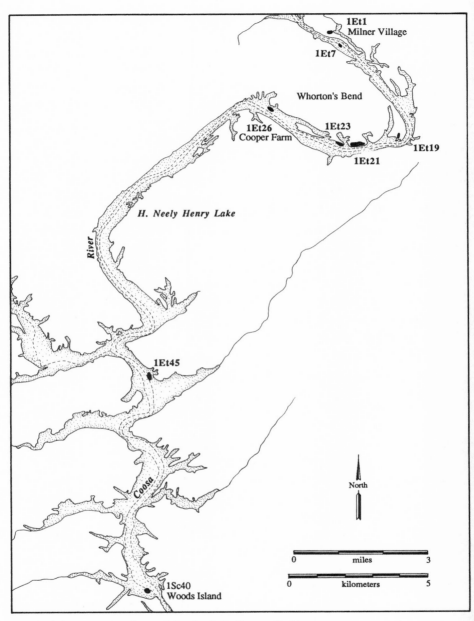

24. Gadsden area site cluster. Map by Julie Barnes Smith.

1969, 1972; Greer 1966; Humbard and Humbard 1965; Lindsey 1964).
Thus, the distribution of sites in this area is relatively well understood,
although reported excavations, other than salvaged burials, are limited.

The Whorton's Bend site cluster consists of six sites, while another
possible site of this period, 1Et45 (1.65 ha), is just downstream. The
Milner village 1Et1 (2.7 ha), Cooper Farm 1Et26, and Site 1Et21 appear
to have been villages, while sites Et7, Et19, and Et23 appear to have been
small hamlets or farmsteads. (The state archaeological site files list Cooper Farm 1Et26 as approximately 0.68 ha, but apparently it is much
larger, according to informants who later salvaged burials. The Alabama
state site files list site 1Et21 as 16 ha, but this multicomponent site was
probably much smaller in the seventeenth century. Informants stated that
it appeared to be smaller than the nearby Cooper Farm site.) Together,
these sites form an almost continuous occupation around Whorton's
Bend. The cluster measures 8.2 km long (14.2 km if 1Et45 is included).
Apparently, there are three main villages, but there are fewer small sites
known for the Whorton's Bend cluster when compared with the Weiss
Reservoir cluster. Again, we might suggest that these three villages represent the amalgamated populations of the three sixteenth-century site clusters in northwest Georgia. Each site of the seventeenth century could
correspond to one of the site clusters of the sixteenth century. Thus, one
site was probably Coosa (from the Coosawattee cluster), one site was
Itaba (from the Cartersville cluster), and the third site may have been
Abihka (or Ulibahali) from the Rome cluster. It can be further hypoth-
esized that the inhabitants of the Bradford Ferry site moved to the Milner
Village. This supposition is based on their location on the same side of the
Coosa River, as opposed to the other villages on the opposite shore. Un-
fortunately, large collections of pottery, which might show specific char-
acteristics of micro-ceramic traditions, are not available from the Milner
Village to test this hypothesis.

Aboriginal ceramics again show a major change from the earlier Weiss
site pottery assemblage. The Weiss sites had a preponderance of plain
surface treatment of vessels, but nearly a third of the sherds recovered
from the Whorton's Bend sites have brushed surface treatments (Smith
1989a). Incised forms are still present, and there is some continuity of
motifs with the earlier Weiss sites. Tempering is shell, as seen in the Weiss

sites. This pottery assemblage is so different from the Weiss phase that it should be considered a new phase: the Whorton's Bend phase.

The lack of major excavations at the Whorton's Bend sites again means we have few basic data about subsistence, community patterns, housing, and so forth. Salvaged burials and refuse pits, excavated before modern flotation recovery, provide the limited data available. Recently analyzed collections from the Milner Village site, excavated in 1948, indicate reliance on deer and bear, but zooarchaeologist Susan Scott has also identified bones of at least two bison (Smith et al. 1993). Rostlund (1960) suggests that bison migrated into the Southeast during the historic period to occupy the old fields of abandoned Indian towns.

The Milner Village residents were clearly bison hunters, showing a major change in subsistence. How much they relied on bison remains to be determined, but the two bison in the limited collections from the site suggest that a significant amount of bison meat was available. Although plant remains from the Whorton's Bend cluster are lacking, it is likely that some European plants, such as peaches, were also grown by this time.

Burials were excavated at the Cooper Farm and Milner village sites (fig. 25). European trade material was abundant, and aboriginal goods, such as pottery vessels, still appeared in graves. Eyed iron axes (that is, those with an oval or circular eye for hafting) were popular for the first time. Although an eyed axe first appeared in the Coosa sequence at the Seven Springs site of the Weiss cluster (early seventeenth century), iron chisel or celt blades were more common. An eyed axe could be sawn apart, making two or three chisel blades. Evidence of this practice is seen at the late sixteenth-century Polecat Ford site (1Ce308) (Collections at Moundville, Alabama) and has also been documented from historic sites in the Guntersville Basin in northern Alabama (Fleming and Walthall 1978). This evidence suggests that iron was rare, or that the ancient native hafting technique of wedging the celt blade into a slot in the wooden handle was preferred to the new European style of forcing the handle into the formed eye of the axe. By the mid-seventeenth century, eyed axes were common grave goods, suggesting that metal tools were no longer difficult to obtain or that the new hafting style had been accepted. At the sixteenth-century King site, iron celts were clearly hoarded by the elite of the town, some having multiple examples (Smith 1987). However, graves in

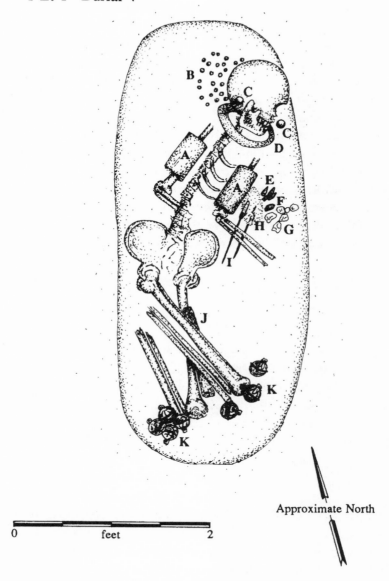

25. Milner village burial. *A*, brass arm band; *B*, blue glass beads; *C*, small brass cones; *D*, brass collar; *E*, projectile points; *F*, galena; *G*, flint spalls and pebbles; *H*, red paint; *I*, iron pins with cane and/or bone handles; *J*, steel knife (under legs); *K*, brass bells. Drawing by Julie Barnes Smith.

the Whorton's Bend area suggest that axes were no longer exotic grave goods. Extreme wear seen on some examples indicates their use as common tools.

Glass beads were common in graves. Sewn beadwork using small glass seed beads was common. Brass discs of the small hole variety and armbands were frequent grave accompaniments, and a new style of brass ornament, the brass collar, appears (plate 5). Small brass clips were affixed to leather clothing, and sheet brass animal effigy pendants were popular. Cast brass harness bells were numerous (plate 5). Absent from these sites are gun parts and glass bottle fragments, but iron knives are commonly found. Sixty-four percent of the twenty-five burials reported from Cooper Farm contained European artifacts.

Native grave goods include flint arrow points, pottery vessels, stone pipes (plate 6a), pigments such as red ochre and galena, and stone-workers' tool caches. Such caches include flint raw material, hammer stones, abraders, and sometimes bone or beaver-tooth tools. Ground stone tools, such as stone axes, are absent, but the same tool-making technology is still used in the manufacture of discoidal stones and stone pipes.

One interesting artifact recovered from a burial at the Whorton's Bend site (1Et21) or immediately adjacent to it is a large copper celt. It is a so-called Tukabahchee plate (plate 6b) as illustrated by eighteenth-century Indian trader James Adair (1930:188; Greer 1966). This artifact indicates high status and may signal a revitalization of native values. This trend is also seen in the return of native-made shell beads and earpins in the assemblage from nearby Cooper Farm.

Woods Island (ca. 1670–1715)

By about 1670, the Coosa River people again moved downstream, this time stopping to form a large town on Woods Island, 18 linear km downstream from Whorton's Bend (see fig. 22). Today the entire stretch of the Coosa River from Gadsden to Logan Martin Lake is a series of reservoirs. An archaeological survey was done in conjunction with the construction of each of these reservoirs. Despite all this research, sites of the late seventeenth century are rare. Only the large (10.4 ha) Woods Island site and a nearby small farmstead site, 1Sc46, have been located in the area.

The next nearest possible historic-period site that has had any investigation is the Williams site, 1Ta200 (Hubbert and Ray n.d.), in Talledega County, 18.25 linear km to the south of Woods Island. This site is relatively isolated and, based on pottery styles, is probably not contemporary with Woods Island. None of the three features excavated, including a burial, contained any possible European artifacts except a piece of copper.

The founding of one large site at Woods Island apparently indicates that the three villages and several farmsteads of the Whorton's Bend cluster had amalgamated into one large village sometime close to A.D. 1670. It was about then that slave-raiding Indians, armed with English firearms, began pressuring interior peoples. Charleston was founded in 1670, and the Indian slave trade quickly grew. The aboriginal groups in the Southeast not armed with guns were at the mercy of groups who had European weapons. An island location could provide some measure of security. The acquisition of firearms quickly became a survival issue. At Woods Island, for the first time in the Coosa River sequence, flintlock gun parts, lead shot, and gunflints are found. A late seventeenth-century English sword (plate 7a) attests to contact with English traders, and Crane (1981:46) states that an English trading post was established among the Abihka in the last years of the seventeenth century.

It is possible that Thomas Nairne passed through the Woods Island town in 1708, but he does not describe it in his journals (Moore 1988). Nairne does mention the Obechas (Abihkas) in passing, perhaps indicating that the main town of the Coosa River—that is, the Woods Island site—was known as Abihka in 1708. However, he later mentions going from "Cusa" to the Chickasaws, indicating the presence of a Coosa town. It is likely that both Abihkas and Coosas lived in the Woods Island town; they may have maintained separate identities (Smith 1995).

By 1707 the Abihka (Abecau) Nation is listed as one of five divisions of the Creek towns recognized by the English (Crane 1981:83). By this time, Abihka town had clearly eclipsed Coosa in importance. Again, it is likely that Woods Island was the Abihka town of this period. In 1714 the Abihkas joined an English expedition against the Choctaws to force them into the English trade network (Crane 1981:104). From this time until removal in the 1830s (and afterward in Oklahoma), the Abihka were a powerful force in the Creek Confederacy.

Aboriginal pottery at Woods Island consists almost entirely of shell-tempered plain wares. Brushed pottery continued to be important, but it decreased to only 12.3 percent of the sherds. Shell-tempered cordmarked pottery sherds appear in some quantity for the first time (3.5 percent), a change that might signal the movement of Tennessee River Koasati-speaking groups into the area from the Guntersville Basin region of the Tennessee River. In 1686, Marcos Delgado documents the movement of northern Muskogean groups (which included the Koasati) to the south (Boyd 1937), fleeing armed Indian slave raiders. The sudden appearance of cordmarked pottery probably reflects this migration, since it was a common pottery decoration on archaeological sites on the Tennessee River.

Subsistence at Woods Island is poorly known because archaeological work was conducted before the use of modern flotation techniques, but maize, beans, squash, and peaches were recovered. The presence of peaches at Woods Island signals the first time that an Old World plant has appeared in the Coosa River sequence, but it may be due to biases of excavation and analysis techniques. Animal bones identified at Woods Island include deer, turtle, and small mammal (Morrell 1965).

For the first time in the Coosa River sequence since the sixteenth century, data on dwellings are available. In three seasons at Woods Island, seven houses or partial houses were recorded (Morrell 1965; Graham 1966; Joseph Benthal field notes on file at Moundville). Approximate measurements (in feet) for five complete houses are 15 × 15, 15 × 10, 14 × 14, 16 × 10, and 22 × 12. While some of the structures are square, others are decidedly rectangular. All are small compared to houses excavated at the sixteenth-century King site. The average floor area for houses at Woods Island is only 199 square feet while the earlier King site houses averaged 684 square feet (based on measurements in Smith 1987). Virtually all the King site structures are square or nearly so, so a change in house shape is also indicated. Assuming that house size is a measure of family size or population in general (Ramenofsky 1987; Smith 1987), the Woods Island data indicate a severe loss of population.

There also appears to be a more dispersed distribution of houses at Woods Island than at the King site, signaling a change in settlement. At Woods Island, the average distance between the nearest neighboring houses in a block excavation is 81 feet, but King site houses are never more than 35 feet from an adjacent house. Again, per unit of site area, Woods Island has fewer and smaller houses, presenting a low density of population compared to the sixteenth-century King site.

Although Woods Island is large at 10.4 ha (compared to 2 ha for the King site or 4.9 ha for Little Egypt), the population may not have been large because of the dispersed nature of settlement. By using the number of houses observed in a large excavated area and projecting it over the entire site, we can estimate a total of forty-six houses — a number virtually identical to the forty-seven houses estimated for the King site (Hally 1988). Note that this is the only village of this period in the area whereas the previous site cluster contained three villages and several farmsteads.

Forty-eight burials were recorded during investigations at Woods Island (Morrell 1965; Smith 1989a). Of these burials, data on grave accompaniments are available for forty-one. Ten burials contained no grave goods. Four were extended burials, and at least two were in stone box graves, suggesting that they date to an earlier component (perhaps the Etowah Culture occupation) of the site. An additional extended burial was accompanied by three shell beads and is also probably an early burial. The remaining flexed burials without grave goods might belong to the historic occupation.

Of the thirty burials with grave goods that appear to date to the historic period, only two did not have European trade objects. One of these burials contained only a stone projectile point. The other contained a shell-tempered pot but had been vandalized by pot hunters, so complete data on grave goods are not available. Twenty-eight burials contained European objects, including abundant glass beads (plate 7b), brass disc and crescent ornaments, brass arm bands, iron axes, brass harness bells (plate 8a), knives, and buttons. The buttons perhaps suggest the presence of European clothing, but this is not clear from descriptions of their locations in the graves. Many Native American groups also used buttons as ornaments. New types of European grave goods included a brass kettle, iron hoes of the Spanish lugged type (plate 8b), and gun parts in at least two burials. A sword (not seen since the mid-sixteenth century) and scissors were also included. New styles of glass beads appeared, including wire-wound faceted beads, white elongated necklace beads, cornaline d'Aleppo necklace beads (brick red with a green core layer), and new varieties of striped beads (plate 7b). Native-made goods occasionally continued to be included in graves. Four graves contained pottery vessels, and an additional vessel fragment was recorded for another burial. Chipped stone projectile points were present, as were steatite and ceramic tobacco pipes. In general, the use of aboriginal materials as grave accompaniments was on the wane.

On archaeological grounds, it is believed that the Woods Island settlement was abandoned about 1715, perhaps as a result of the settlement shifts that followed the end of the Yamasee War. Indeed, Verner Crane (1981:169) mentions that the Abihkas killed or forced the English traders to flee. Thus, they were clearly part of this general revolt. However, Swanton (1922:253) notes that according to South Carolina colonial records, the Abihka suffered a severe defeat at the hands of the Cherokee in 1716. It is possible that Woods Island was the principal Abihka town of the time and that this defeat was the reason for the abandonment of the Woods Island settlement.

Gatschet (1901:402) believed that Coosa may have once been part of the neighboring Abihka town. This picture fits the known archaeology, which suggests that the remnants of the Coosa chiefdom amalgamated into the large Woods Island site, only to separate into two or more towns in the early eighteenth century.

A 1715 census lists a population of 502 men or 1,773 people in fifteen Abihka towns, a group that Swanton (1922:431) believes includes the Coosa people also. The 1715 census count of fifteen towns appears confusing since there only appears to be one large archaeological site of this period. However, many eighteenth-century writers label all towns on the Coosa River from the vicinity of Woods Island or Childersburg down to the junction of the Coosa and Tallapoosa Rivers *and* the towns on the upper Tallapoosa River as the Abihkas. The purpose here is to trace the original Coosa-Abihka towns through time. Therefore, I use the name Abihka to indicate an individual town, a usage not common in the eighteenth century. Thus, while many allied towns were said to be occupied by Abihkas in the eighteenth century, we are primarily interested in the one town that was a lineal descendant of sixteenth-century Apica. I believe that this town was located on Woods Island during the period ca. 1670–1715.

There is some evidence from the Barnwell map of ca. 1722 that the Woods Island site was the Abihka town. Barnwell shows Coosa south of

"Habiquechee." Habiquechee is clearly Abihkutci (Little Abihka) of later eighteenth-century maps. (Barnwell also spells Alabama as "Halbama.") Later eighteenth-century maps show Abihkutci south of Coosa. Barnwell's map appears to depict Coosa at its known eighteenth-century location at the Childersburg archaeological site overlooking the junction of Talladega Creek with the Coosa River (see discussion in chapter 4). Thus, his Habiquechee is located to the north, where the trading path crosses the Coosa River. There was an important ford near Woods Island known in the nineteenth century as Ten Island Ford or Jackson's Ford (Hanvey, Hood, and McElroy 1990, 1992). It is likely that this ford was used for the earlier English trading path to the Chickasaws.

For whatever reason, early in the eighteenth century the people of the Coosa River abandoned the Woods Island site and again migrated south, next stopping near present-day Childersburg, Alabama (see fig. 22), in Talledega County. Large groups settled on Talladega and Tallaseehatchee creeks. It is in this location that we again find English and French historic references and maps showing the locations of the Coosa and Abihka towns. This area was the location of the Talisi towns of the sixteenth century, according to research by Charles Hudson and his associates (DePratter, Hudson, and Smith 1985). There is some archaeological evidence, in the form of sites of the Kymulga phase (Knight et al. 1984), that the area was occupied during the period of the sixteenth through the eighteenth centuries. It is probable that the Coosa-Abihka towns joined an existing group of people, the Talisi or the archaeological Kymulga phase, to form one of their last major clusters of towns before removal.

Thus it is believed that the location of the sixteenth-century towns of the Paramount Chiefdom of Coosa have been successfully traced through time, using archaeological methods, to the documented locations of the eighteenth century. The tie between the protohistoric period and the fully historic period has been completed.

7

Summary and Conclusions

The paramount chiefdom of Coosa had a short history. It must have ascended to power after the fall of Etowah in the fourteenth century, spreading its influence and power from east-central Tennessee to east-central Alabama. It was apparently at the height of its power when Hernando de Soto entered the area in 1540. The de Soto chroniclers tell us that numerous towns were subject to Coosa, and its fame had spread to a large area of the Southeast. The later expeditions of Tristán de Luna and Juan Pardo yielded further information about Coosa. By Luna's day (1560), Coosa was on the decline, and one of its tributaries, the Napochies, was rebelling. However, the limited information available from the Pardo expedition (1568) suggests that Coosa still held some authority over the people of eastern Tennessee. None of these narratives suggest that the central towns of Coosa had moved during the twenty-eight years of intermittent Spanish contact.

Following the Spanish expeditions of the mid-sixteenth century, Coosa vanishes from historical records until around 1700. The archaeology of the region suggests that dramatic changes took place during the late sixteenth and seventeenth centuries. The number of towns drastically decreased and houses were spaced farther apart in the remaining towns. Many towns were smaller than their predecessors, and individual houses also decreased in size. Graves containing more than one individual were common. These facts suggest massive depopulation. This was probably due to the effects of European disease epidemics, starvation brought about by the Spaniards' theft of stored food supplies, interruption of planting and harvesting cycles, and outright murder of Indians by Spaniards. These possible epidemics, or the other factors, caused the Coosa people to abandon their traditional homeland and migrate down the Coosa River. New movements were made about every third of a century. This resulted in clusters of towns in the Weiss Reservoir area in the early seventeenth century, the present Gadsden, Alabama, area in the mid-seventeenth century, the Woods Island settlement in the late seventeenth century, and the final settlement in the present Childersburg, Alabama, area in the eighteenth century.

There is also evidence of sociopolitical change. Earthen temple mounds were no longer constructed, suggesting both a shortage of labor and a lack of centralized leadership following the population loss. Crafting of native luxury goods quickly ceased, and we no longer find elite cemetery areas. This suggests that the social positions they once symbolized no longer existed and the elite could no longer support craft specialists.

Site hierarchies of multi-mound centers, secondary administrative centers, and villages devolved into simple village, hamlet, or farmstead settlements. Indeed, there was a definite centripetal effect on settlement. Much of the population dispersed into hamlets and farmsteads for the first time in several hundred years.

Central authority clearly had weakened by the early seventeenth century, and a chiefdom type of political organization probably was no longer in operation. Out of this collapse arose a system of weaker local micos who could only act in conjunction with a town council. That the micos often came from a particular clan was probably a vestige of the earlier system where the position of chief was inherited in one lineage.

As the political organization transformed, so did the social dimensions of the Coosa-Abihka world. Society became more egalitarian as inherited social status gave way to a system of status achieved by hard work or skill in hunting, warfare, and other tasks.

The Coosa natives came to rely more and more on European technology and subsistence practices. Metal tools quickly replaced their stone counterparts. By the end of the seventeenth century some Coosa Indians had firearms. About this same time, we find evidence of European plants (peaches) in the sites, and by the mid-eighteenth century, the natives were relying on chickens and probably cattle and hogs. They quickly became linked to the world economic system as suppliers of leather and furs.

Sometime during these massive transformations, the small town of Apica, recorded by Luna's forces, became the important Abihka of the eighteenth century. My contention is that the Woods Island settlement was already known as Abihka when Englishmen arrived in the late seventeenth century. The Abihkas became an important force in the Creek Confederacy, being one of the founding towns. A Coosa town remained nearly until the time of removal, although clearly in a diminished status. The cycle of rise and fall of the Coosa Paramount Chiefdom was complete.

Throughout all of these changes, the Coosa people managed to maintain their residence within the Ridge and Valley physiographic province. After hundreds if not thousands of years of continually refining their adaptation to this environment, they were not about to give it up, despite the pressures of disease and, eventually, encroaching Europeans. While massive population movements took place, the majority of these remained within the Ridge and Valley. Although their lifeways changed over the centuries from hunting and gathering to horticulture and finally to commercial hunting and stock raising, the Coosa-Abihka people chose to stay in the land they knew. Their homeland was the one largely unchanged factor in their lives. It was a constant they maintained until their forced removal by the United States military in the early nineteenth century.

The story of Indian removal is well known (Foreman 1952; Green 1982; Wright 1986). The new American nation, with its ideology of manifest destiny, relentlessly pushed westward. By the early nineteenth century, the southern white establishment determined that the southeastern Indians must be removed. Their farmland was inviting, and the discovery of gold in the Cherokee lands of northern Georgia sealed the Indians' fate. By the late 1830s, very few Native Americans remained in the Creek country, most having moved to Indian Territory (today's Oklahoma). A few Upper Creeks managed to hold on to their lands, and today the Poarch Band of Creeks remains in Alabama.

One thing this study reveals is the amazing tenacity of the Coosa-Abihka people. Despite population collapse, social and political transformations brought about by European contact, nearly constant warfare with the Choctaw, Cherokee, and Europeans, and erosion of their territory, they remained a viable entity. Indeed, the Abihka remained a significant force after Indian removal to Oklahoma in the 1830s, where their descendants continue to live today.

There is still need for much research on the Coosa people. A few of their towns may lie outside the confines of reservoirs, and excavation with modern techniques could answer many questions about changing health and subsistence. The virtual lack of late sixteenth-century towns is particularly problematical. It is possible that the decimation caused by introduced disease was so extensive that only one town remained. However, more survey work must be done to confirm the absence of late sixteenth-century towns in the region. Additional analysis of the large collections from Woods Island and the Childersburg site should offer much new data, but the modern excavation of the eighteenth-century Abihka town would be more rewarding. The archaeology of the late eighteenth and early nineteenth century Coosa people is virtually unknown, yet the archaeological sites are known and could be explored. Finally, additional archaeological research into the Abihka towns in Oklahoma would provide information on how these people adapted to their new environment when they finally left their Ridge and Valley home.

References

Adair, James
1930   *History of the American Indians*. Reprinted, Promontory Press, New York. Originally published by National Society of Colonial Dames of America, Tennessee.

Anderson, David
1990   *Political Change in Chiefdom Societies: Cycling in the Late Prehistoric Southeastern United States*. Ph.D. diss., University of Michigan. University Microfilms, Ann Arbor.

1994   *The Savannah River Chiefdoms*. University of Alabama Press, Tuscaloosa.

Anderson, David, Jerald Ledbetter, and Lisa O'Steen
1990   *Paleoindian Period Archaeology of Georgia*. Laboratory of Archaeology Series, Report No. 22. University of Georgia, Athens.

Anonymous
1963   *Archaeological Investigations of the Logan Martin Dam Reservoir in Talladega and St. Clair Counties, June 1, 1963–September 1, 1963*. Progress report submitted to the Alabama Power Company by the Department of Sociology and Anthropology, University of Alabama, Moundville.

1964   *Archaeological Investigations of the Lock Three Dam Reservoir in Etowah and St. Clair Counties, Alabama, January 1, 1964–December 31, 1964*. Progress report submitted to the Alabama Power Company by the Department of Sociology and Anthropology, University of Alabama, Moundville.

1965   *Archaeological Investigations in the Lock Three Dam Reservoir in Calhoun, Etowah, and St. Clair Counties, Alabama, January 1, 1965–December 31, 1965*. Final progress report submitted to the Alabama Power Company by the Department of Sociology and Anthropology, University of Alabama, Moundville.

Avellaneda, Ignacio
1990   Los Sobrevivientes de la Florida: The Survivors of the De Soto Expedition. Research publications of the P. K. Yonge Library of Florida History No. 2. University of Florida, Gainesville.

Bartram, William
1853   Observations on the Creek and Cherokee Indians, 1789. Transactions of the American Ethnological Society 3:1–81.
1928   Travels of William Bartram. Dover Publications, New York.

Battles, Mrs. Richard E. [Juanita]
1969   One Foot in a Grave. Journal of Alabama Archaeology 15(1):35–38.
1972   Copper and Lithic Artifacts. Journal of Alabama Archaeology 18:32–35.

Beck, Robin A., Jr.
1997   From Joara to Chiaha: Spanish Exploration of the Appalachian Summit Area, 1540–1568. Southeastern Archaeology 16:162–69.

Blakely, Robert, ed.
1988   The King Site: Continuity and Contact in Sixteenth-Century Georgia. University of Georgia Press, Athens.

Bogan, Arthur
1987   Faunal Analysis. In The Toqua Site: A Late Mississippian Dallas Phase Town, edited by Richard Polhemus, 971–1112. Tennessee Valley Authority Publications in Anthropology No. 44. University of Tennessee, Knoxville.

Booker, Karen, Charles Hudson, and Robert Rankin
1992   Place Names Identification and Multilingualism in the Sixteenth-Century Southeast. Ethnohistory 39:399–451.

Boyd, Mark F.
1937   Expedition of Marcos Delgado, 1686. Florida Historical Quarterly 16:2–32.

Brain, Jeffrey P.
1979   Tunica Treasure. Papers of the Peabody Museum of American Archaeology and Ethnology No. 71. Harvard University Press, Cambridge.
1985   Introduction: Update of De Soto Studies since the United States De Soto Expedition Commission Report. In Final Report of the United States De Soto Expedition Commission, edited by John R. Swanton, xi–lxxii. Smithsonian Institution Press, Washington, D.C.

Brain, Jeffrey P., and Philip Phillips
1996   Shell Gorgets. Peabody Museum Press, Cambridge, Massachusetts.

Braun, E. Lucy
1950   Deciduous Forests of Eastern North America. Bleakston Company, Philadelphia.

Brown, Ian
1979   Bells. In Tunica Treasure, edited by Jeffrey P. Brain, 197–205. Papers of the Peabody Museum of American Archaeology and Ethnology No. 71. Harvard University Press, Cambridge.

Brown, James A.

1976 The Southern Cult Reconsidered. *Midcontinental Journal of Archaeology* 1:115–36.

Caldwell, Joseph R.

1958 *Trend and Tradition in the Prehistory of the Eastern United States.* Memoir of the American Anthropological Association No. 88. Springfield, Illinois.

1964 Interaction Spheres in Prehistory. In *Hopewellian Studies,* edited by Joseph Caldwell and Robert Hall, 133–43. Scientific Papers No. 12. Illinois State Museum, Springfield.

Clayton, Lawrence, Vernon J. Knight, and Edward Moore

1993 *The De Soto Chronicles.* 2 vols. University of Alabama Press, Tuscaloosa.

Cobb, Charles, and Patrick Garrow

1996 Woodstock Culture and the Question of Mississippian Emergence. *American Antiquity* 61:21–37.

Cook, Sherburne F.

1972 *Prehistoric Demography.* Addison-Wesley Module in Anthropology 16. Addison-Wesley, Reading, Massachusetts.

Corkran, David

1967 *The Creek Frontier, 1540–1783.* University of Oklahoma Press, Norman.

Coxe, Daniel

1976 [1722] *A Description of the English Province of Carolana, By the Spaniards call'd Florida, And by the French La Louisiane.* 1976 facsimile ed. University of Florida Press, Gainesville.

Crane, Verner

1981 *The Southern Frontier: 1670–1732.* W. W. Norton, New York.

Deagan, Kathleen

1987 *Artifacts of the Spanish Colonies,* vol. 1. Smithsonian Institution Press, Washington, D.C.

DeJarnette, David, and Asael T. Hansen

1960 *The Archaeology of the Childersburg Site, Alabama.* Notes in Anthropology No. 4. Florida State University, Tallahassee.

DeJarnette, David, Edward Kurjack, and Bennie Keel

1973 Archaeological Investigations in the Weiss Reservoir of the Coosa River in Alabama. *Journal of Alabama Archaeology* 19:1–201.

DePratter, Chester B.

1983 *Late Prehistoric and Early Historic Chiefdoms in the Southeastern United States.* Ph.D. diss., University of Georgia. University Microfilms, Ann Arbor.

1994 The Chiefdom of Cofitachequi. In *The Forgotten Centuries: Indians and Europeans in the American South, 1521–1704,* edited by Charles Hudson and Carmen Chaves Tesser, 197–226. University of Georgia Press, Athens.

DePratter, Chester B., and Marvin T. Smith

1980 Sixteenth Century European Trade in the Southeastern United States: Evidence from the Juan Pardo Expeditions (1566–1568). In *Spanish Colonial Frontier Research*, edited by Henry F. Dobyns, 67–78. Center for Anthropological Studies, Albuquerque.

DePratter, Chester B., Charles Hudson, and Marvin T. Smith

1983   The Route of Juan Pardo's Explorations in the Interior Southeast, 1566–1568. *Florida Historical Quarterly* 62:125–58.

1985   The De Soto Expedition: From Chiaha to Mabila. In *Alabama and the Borderlands, from Prehistory to Statehood*, edited by Reid Badger and Lawrence Clayton, 108–27. University of Alabama Press, Tuscaloosa.

Dobyns, Henry

1983   *Their Number Become Thinned*. University of Tennessee Press, Knoxville.

du Pratz, Antoine S. Le Page

1774   *History of Louisiana*. 3 vols. London.

Elvas, Gentleman of

1968   *Narratives of De Soto in the Conquest of Florida*. Palmetto Books, Gainesville, Florida.

Fiedel, Stuart

1999   Older Than We Thought: Implications of Corrected Dates for Paleoindians. *American Antiquity* 64(1):95–115.

Fleming, Victor K., and John Walthall

1978   A Summary of the Historic Aboriginal Occupations of the Guntersville Basin, Alabama. *Southeastern Archaeological Conference Special Publication* 5:30–34.

Foreman, Grant

1952   *Indian Removal: The Emigration of the Five Civilized Tribes*. University of Oklahoma Press, Norman.

Gatschet, Albert S.

1901   Towns and Villages of the Creek Confederacy in the XVIII and XIX Centuries. *Publications of the Alabama Historical Society, Miscellaneous Collections* 1:386–415. Alabama Historical Society, Montgomery.

Graham, J. Bennett

1966   An Archaeological Local Sequence Chronology in the Lock 3 Reservoir. M.A. thesis, University of Alabama, Tuscaloosa.

Green, Michael D.

1982   *The Politics of Indian Removal: Creek Government and Society in Crisis*. University of Nebraska Press, Lincoln.

Greer, E. S.

1966   A Tukabahchee Plate from the Coosa River. *Journal of Alabama Archaeology* 12:156–58.

Hally, David J.

1970   *Archaeological Investigation of the Potts' Tract Site (9Mu103), Carters Dam, Murray County, Georgia*. Laboratory of Archaeology Series, Report No. 6. University of Georgia, Athens.

1975   Introduction to the Symposium: The King Site and Its Investigation. *Southeastern Archaeological Conference Bulletin* 18:48–54.

1979   *Archaeological Investigations of the Little Egypt Site (9Mu102), Murray County, Ga., 1969 Season.* Laboratory of Archaeology Series Report No. 18. University of Georgia, Athens.

1980   *Archaeological Investigation of the Little Egypt Site (9Mu102), Murray County, Ga., 1970–72 Seasons.* Submitted to the Heritage Conservation and Recreation Service, U.S. Department of the Interior, contract nos. 14-10-9-900-390, 1910P21041, 9911T000411, C5546.

1981   Plant Preservation and the Content of Paleobotanical Samples: A Case Study. *American Antiquity* 46:723–42.

1983   The Interpretive Potential of Pottery from Domestic Contexts. *Midcontinental Journal of Archaeology* 8:163–96.

1985   Regional Variants of Lamar Culture. Paper presented at the Society of Georgia Archaeology, Athens.

1988   Archaeology and Settlement Plan of the King Site. In *The King Site: Continuity and Contact in Sixteenth-Century Georgia*, edited by Robert Blakely, 3–16. University of Georgia Press, Athens.

1994   The Chiefdom of Coosa. In *The Forgotten Centuries: Indians and Europeans in the American South, 1521–1704*, edited by Charles Hudson and Carmen Chaves Tesser, 227–53. University of Georgia Press, Athens.

Hally, David J., and Hypatia Kelly

1998   The Nature of Mississippian Towns in Georgia: The King Site Example. In *Mississippian Towns and Sacred Spaces*, edited by R. Barry Lewis and Charles Stout, 49–63. University of Alabama Press, Tuscaloosa.

Hally, David J., and James B. Langford

1988   *Mississippi Period Archaeology of the Georgia Valley and Ridge Province.* Laboratory of Archaeology Series Report No. 25. University of Georgia, Athens.

Hally, David J., Marvin T. Smith, and James B. Langford

1990   The Archaeological Reality of De Soto's Coosa. In *Columbian Consequences*, vol. 2, *Archaeological and Historical Perspectives on the Spanish Borderlands East*, edited by David Hurst Thomas, 121–38. Smithsonian Institution Press, Washington, D.C.

Hanvey, Patsy, Charlotte Hood, and Bette Sue McElroy

1990   Historic Ten Islands: Alabama's Hidden Treasure. Report prepared for the Alabama Power Company.

1992   Ten Islands of the Coosa River. *Journal of Alabama Archaeology* 38:171–82.

Hawkins, Benjamin

1848   *A Sketch of the Creek Country, in 1798 and 1799.* Georgia Historical Society Collections, vol. 3. Georgia Historical Society, Savannah.

Holstein, Harry O., and Keith Little

ca. 1986 *A Short-Term Archaeological Investigation of the Davis Farm Archaeological Complex, a Multicomponent Prehistoric Site in Calhoun County, Alabama.* Archaeological Resource Laboratory Research Series 1. Jacksonville State University, Jacksonville, Alabama.

Holstein, Harry O., Curtis Hill, and Keith Little

1997 The Hurley Site (1Ce137): A Protohistoric Habitation Site in the Weiss Lake Basin, Cherokee County, Alabama. *Journal of Alabama Archaeology* 43:1–34.

Holstein, Harry O., Curtis Hill, Keith Little, and Caleb Curren

1990 Ethnohistoric Archaeology and Hypothesis Testing: Archaeological Investigation of the Terrapin Creek Site. Draft report submitted to the Alabama De Soto Commission, Tuscaloosa.

Holstein, Harry O., Keith Little, Curtis Hill, and Caleb Curren

1992 In Search of De Luna's Coosa. Paper presented at the 57th annual meeting, Society for American Archaeology, Pittsburgh.

Hubbert, Charles, and Craig Ray

n.d. The Williams Site (Ta200). Manuscript on file at Mound State Monument, Moundville, Alabama.

Hudson, Charles M., Jr.

1976 *The Southeastern Indians.* University of Tennessee Press, Knoxville.

1979 *Black Drink: A Native American Tea.* University of Georgia Press, Athens.

1988 A Spanish-Coosa Alliance in Sixteenth-Century North Georgia. *Georgia Historical Quarterly* 72:599–626.

1990a A Synopsis of the Hernando de Soto Expedition, 1539–1543. In *De Soto Trail National Historic Trail Study Final Report*, 75–126. National Park Service Southeast Regional Office.

1990b *The Juan Pardo Expeditions.* Smithsonian Institution Press, Washington, D.C.

1997 *Knights of Spain, Warriors of the Sun.* University of Georgia Press, Athens.

Hudson, Charles, Marvin T. Smith, Chester DePratter, and Emilia Kelley

1989 The Tristán de Luna Expedition, 1559–1561. *Southeastern Archaeology* 8(1):31–45.

Hudson, Charles, Marvin Smith, David J. Hally, Richard Polhemus, and Chester B. DePratter

1985 Coosa: A Chiefdom in the Sixteenth-Century Southeastern United States. *American Antiquity* 50:723–37.

Humbard, Richard, and John Humbard

1965 Burial Caches. *Journal of Alabama Archaeology* 11:133–42.

Jefferies, Richard W.

1976 *The Tunacunnhee Site.* Anthropological Paper No. 1. University of Georgia, Athens.

Jones, Charles C., Jr.
1861 *Monumental Remains of Georgia.* John M. Cooper and Co., Savannah, Georgia.

Kelly, Arthur R.
1970 *Explorations at Bell Field Mound and Village Seasons 1965, 1966, 1967, 1968.* Report submitted to National Park Service. On file, Laboratory of Archaeology, University of Georgia, Athens.
1976 9MU104, A Multi-Unit Woodland Site at Carter's Dam, Georgia. *Southeastern Archaeological Conference Bulletin* 19:3–5.

Kelly, Arthur, Frank Schnell, Donald Smith, and Ann Schlosser
1965 *Explorations in Sixtoe Field, Carter's Dam, Murray County, Georgia, Seasons of 1962, 1963, 1964.* Report submitted to the National Park Service.

King, Adam
1997 A New Perspective on the Etowah Valley Mississippian Ceramic Sequence. *Early Georgia* 25(2):36–61.

Knight, Vernon J.
1985a *Tukabatchee: Archaeological Investigations at an Historic Creek Town, Elmore County, Alabama, 1984.* Report of Investigations No. 45. Office of Archaeological Research, Alabama State Museum of Natural History, University of Alabama, Moundville.
1985b *East Alabama Archaeological Survey 1985 Season.* Report of Investigations No. 47. Office of Archaeological Research, University of Alabama, Moundville.
1986 The Institutional Organization of Mississippian Religion. *American Antiquity* 51:675–87.
1989 Symbolism of Mississippian Mounds. In *Powhatan's Mantle: Indians in the Colonial Southeast*, edited by Peter H. Wood, Gregory Waselkov, and M. Thomas Hatley, 279–91. University of Nebraska Press, Lincoln.
1990 Social Organization and the Evolution of Hierarchy in Southeastern Chiefdoms. *Journal of Anthropological Research* 46:1–23.
1994 The Formation of the Creeks. In *The Forgotten Centuries: Indians and Europeans in the American South, 1521–1704*, edited by Charles Hudson and Carmen Chaves Tesser, 373–92. University of Georgia Press, Athens.

Knight, Vernon J., and Sheree Adams
1981 A Voyage to the Mobile and Tomen in 1700, with Notes on the Interior of Alabama. *Journal of Alabama Archaeology* 27:32–56.

Knight, Vernon J., Gloria Cole, and Richard Walling
1984 *An Archaeological Reconnaissance of the Coosa and Tallapoosa River Valleys, East Alabama: 1983.* Report of Investigations 43. Office of Archaeological Research, University of Alabama, Moundville.

Kuchler, A. W.
1964 *Potential Natural Vegetation of the Coterminous United States.* Special Publication 36. American Geographical Society, New York.

Langford, James B.
1990   The Coosawattee Plate: A Sixteenth-Century Catholic/Aztec Artifact from Northwest Georgia. In *Columbian Consequences* 2, edited by David H. Thomas, 139–52. Smithsonian Institution Press, Washington, D.C.

Langford, James B., and Marvin T. Smith
1990   Recent Investigations in the Core of the Coosa Province. In *Lamar Archaeology: Mississippian Chiefdoms in the Deep South*, edited by J. Mark Williams and Gary Shapiro, 104–16. University of Alabama Press, Tuscaloosa.

Larson, Lewis H.
1971a Settlement Distribution during the Mississippian Period. *Southeastern Archaeological Conference Bulletin* 13:19–25.
1971b Archaeological Implications of Social Stratification of the Etowah Site, Georgia. In *Approaches to the Social Dimensions of Mortuary Practices*, edited by James A. Brown, 58–67. Memoir 25. Society for American Archaeology.
1972   Functional Considerations of Aboriginal Warfare in the Southeast during the Mississippi Period. *American Antiquity* 37:383–92.
1989   The Etowah Site. In *The Southeastern Ceremonial Complex Artifacts and Analysis*, edited by Patricia Galloway, 133–41. University of Nebraska Press, Lincoln.

Lewis, T.M.N., and Madeline Kneberg
1946   *Hiwassee Island*. University of Tennessee Press, Knoxville.

Lindsey, Mrs. E. M.
1964   Cooper Farm Salvage Project. *Journal of Alabama Archaeology* 10:22–29.

Little, Keith
1985   A Sixteenth Century European Sword from a Proto-historic Aboriginal Site in Northwest Georgia. *Early Georgia* 13:1–14.

Little, Keith, and Cailup B. Curren
1981   Site 1Ce308: A Protohistoric Site on the Upper Coosa River in Alabama. *Journal of Alabama Archaeology* 27:117–24.

Little, Keith, and Caleb Curren
1989   Conquest Archaeology of Alabama. Paper presented at the 54th annual meeting of the Society for American Archaeology, Atlanta.

Mereness, Newton D., ed.
1916   *Travels in the American Colonies, 1690–1783*. Macmillan, Norwood, Massachusetts.

Mistovich, Tim S.
1981a *An Intensive Phase II Cultural Resources Survey of Selected Areas on the Coosa River Navigation Project*, vol. 1. Report of Investigations 20. Office of Archaeological Research, University of Alabama, Moundville.
1981b *An Intensive Phase II Cultural Resources Survey of Selected Areas on the Coosa River Navigation Project*, vol. 2. Report of Investigations 32. Office of Archaeological Research, University of Alabama, Moundville.

Mistovich, Tim, and David Zeanah

1983a *An Intensive Phase II Cultural Resources Survey of Selected Areas on the Coosa River Navigation Project*, vol. 3. Report of Investigations 35. Office of Archaeological Research, University of Alabama, Moundville.

1983b *An Intensive Phase II Cultural Resources Survey of Selected Areas on the Coosa River Navigation Project*, vol. 4. Report of Investigations 38. Office of Archaeological Research, University of Alabama, Moundville.

Moore, Alexander

1988 *Nairne's Muskhogean Journals.* University Press of Mississippi, Jackson.

Moorehead, Warren K.

1932 *Exploration of the Etowah Site in Georgia.* Etowah Papers 1. Department of Archaeology, Phillips Academy, New Haven.

Morrell, L. Ross

1965 *The Woods Island Site in Southeastern Acculturation, 1625–1800.* Notes in Anthropology 11. Florida State University, Tallahassee.

Myer, William E.

1928 *Indian Trails of the Southeast.* 42d annual report of the Bureau of American Ethnology, 1924–25, 727–857. Bureau of American Ethnology, Washington, D.C.

Naroll, Raoul

1962 Floor Area and Settlement Population. *American Antiquity* 27:587–89.

Peebles, Christopher, and Susan Kus

1977 Some Archaeological Correlates of Ranked Societies. *American Antiquity* 42:421–48.

Pluckhahn, Thomas

1996 Joseph Caldwell's Summerour Mound (9Fo16) and Woodland Platform Mounds in the Southeastern United States. *Southeastern Archaeology* 15:191–210.

Polhemus, Richard

1987 *The Toqua Site: A Late Mississippian Dallas Phase Town.* Report of Investigations 41, Department of Anthropology, University of Tennessee, Knoxville, and Publications in Anthropology 44, Tennessee Valley Authority, Norris.

Priestly, Herbert I.

1928 *The Luna Papers.* Publications of the Florida State Historical Society No. 8. 2 vols. Florida State Historical Society, DeLand.

Ramenofsky, Ann F.

1987 *Vectors of Death.* University of New Mexico Press, Albuquerque.

Ranjel, Rodrigo

1904 Narrative. In *Narratives of the Career of Hernando de Soto,* translated by Edward Gaylord Bourne, 41–149. A. S. Barnes, New York.

Romans, Bernard

1962 *A Concise Natural History of East and West Florida.* Facsimile reproduction of the 1775 edition. University of Florida Press, Gainesville.

Rostlund, Erhard

1960   The Geographic Range of the Historic Bison in the Southeast. *Annals of the Association of American Geographers* 50:395–407.

Roth, Janet

1980   Analysis of Faunal Remains. In *Archaeological Investigation of the Little Egypt Site (9Mu102), Murray County, Georgia, 1970–72 Seasons*, by David J. Hally, 570–91. Submitted to the Heritage Conservation and Recreation Service, U.S. Department of the Interior, contract nos. 14-10-9-900-390, 1910P21041, 9911T000411, C5546. Report on file at the Laboratory of Archaeology, University of Georgia, Athens.

Rowland, Dunbar

1911   *Mississippi Provincial Archives, 1763–1766: English Dominion.* Brandon Printing Company, Nashville, Tennessee.

Rowland, Dunbar, Albert Sanders, and Patricia Galloway

1984a   *Mississippi Provincial Archives, 1729–1740.* Vol. 1. Mississippi Department of Archives and History, Jackson.

1984b   *Mississippi Provincial Archives.* Vol. 11. Mississippi Department of Archives and History, Jackson.

Schnell, Frank T.

1989   The Beginnings of the Creeks: Where Did They First 'Sit Down'? *Early Georgia* 17:24–29.

Shea, Andrea, Richard Polhemus, and Jefferson Chapman

1987   Paleobotany. In *The Toqua Site: A Late Mississippian Dallas Phase Town*, edited by Richard Polhemus, 1113–1208. Tennessee Valley Authority Publications in Anthropology 44. University of Tennessee, Knoxville.

Sheldon, Elisabeth Shepard

1982   *Continuity and Change in Plant Use from the Mississippian to the Historic Period.* Ph.D. diss., University of Alabama. University Microfilms, Ann Arbor.

Smith, Bruce D.

1986   The Archaeology of the Southeastern United States: From Dalton to de Soto, 10,500–500 B.P. In *Advances in World Archaeology*, 5:1–92. Academic Press, Orlando, Florida.

1989   Origins of Agriculture in Eastern North America. *Science* 246:1566–71.

Smith, Buckingham

1968   *Narratives of De Soto.* Palmetto Books, Gainesville, Florida.

Smith, Marvin T.

1977   The Early Historic Period (1540–1670) on the Upper Coosa River Drainage of Alabama and Georgia. *Conference on Historic Site Archaeology Papers, 1976* 11:151–67.

1983   Chronology from Glass Beads: The Spanish Period in the Southeast, 1513–1670. In *Proceedings of the 1982 Glass Trade Bead Conference*, edited by

Charles Hayes, 65–77. Rochester Museum Research Records vol. 16. Rochester, New York.

1987 *Archaeology of Aboriginal Culture Change in the Interior Southeast: Depopulation during the Early Historic Period.* Ripley P. Bullen Monographs in Anthropology and History. University of Florida Press, Gainesville.

1989a *In the Wake of De Soto: Alabama's Seventeenth-Century Indians on the Coosa River.* Report submitted to the Alabama De Soto Commission, Tuscaloosa, Alabama.

1989b Aboriginal Population Movements in the Early Historic Period Interior Southeast. In *Powhatan's Mantle: Indians in the Colonial Southeast,* edited by Peter H. Wood, Gregory Waselkov, and M. Thomas Hatley, 21–34. University of Nebraska Press, Lincoln.

1992 *Historic Period Indian Archaeology of Northern Georgia.* Laboratory of Archaeology Series Report No. 30. University of Georgia, Athens.

1995 Woods Island Revisited. *Journal of Alabama Archaeology* 41:93–106.

Smith, Marvin T., and Mary Elizabeth Good

1982 *Early Sixteenth Century Glass Beads in the Spanish Colonial Trade.* Cottonlandia Museum Publications, Greenwood, Mississippi.

Smith, Marvin T., Vernon J. Knight, Julie B. Smith, and Ken Turner

1993 The Milner Village (1Et1): A Mid Seventeenth Century Site near Gadsden, Alabama. In *Archaeological Survey and Excavations in the Coosa River Valley, Alabama,* edited by Vernon J. Knight, Jr., 49–61. Bulletin 15. Alabama Museum of Natural History, Tuscaloosa.

Spencer, Charles S.

1987 Rethinking the Chiefdom. In *Chiefdoms in the Americas,* edited by Robert Drennan and Carlos Uribe, 369–89. University Press of America, New York.

Steponaitis, Vincas

1978 Location Theory and Complex Chiefdoms: A Mississippian Example. In *Mississippian Settlement Patterns,* edited by Bruce D. Smith, 417–53. Academic Press, New York.

1983 *Ceramics, Chronology, and Community Patterns: An Archaeological Study at Moundville.* Academic Press, New York.

Stowe, Noel R.

1982 *A Preliminary Report on the Pine Log Creek Site 1Ba462.* University of South Alabama Archaeological Research Laboratory, Mobile.

Sullivan, Lynne P.

1987 The Mouse Creek Phase Household. *Southeastern Archaeology* 6:16–29.

Surrey, N. M. Miller

1916 *The Commerce of Louisiana during the French Regime, 1699–1763.* Columbia University Press, New York.

Swanton, John R.

1922 *Early History of the Creek Indians and Their Neighbors.* Bureau of American Ethnology Bulletin No. 73. Smithsonian Institution, Washington, D.C.

1928 *Social Organization and Social Usages of the Indians of the Creek Confederacy.* 42d annual report of the Bureau of American Ethnology, 1924–25. Smithsonian Institution, Washington, D.C.

1939 *Final Report of the United States De Soto Expedition Commission.* House Document 71. 76th Congress, 1st sess. Government Printing Office, Washington, D.C.

1946 *Indians of the Southeastern United States.* Bureau of American Ethnology Bulletin 137. Smithsonian Institution, Washington, D.C.

Varner, John, and Jeannette Varner (translators and editors)

1951 *The Florida of the Inca*, by Garcilaso de la Vega. University of Texas Press, Austin.

Walthall, John A.

1980 *Prehistoric Indians of the Southeast: Archaeology of Alabama and the Middle South.* University of Alabama Press, Tuscaloosa.

Ward, H. Trawick

1985 Social Implications of Storage and Disposal Patterns. In *Structure and Process in Southeastern Archaeology*, edited by Roy S. Dickens and H. Trawick Ward, 82–101. University of Alabama Press, Tuscaloosa.

Waselkov, Gregory

1980 *Coosa River Archaeology.* 2 vols. Auburn University Archaeological Monograph No. 2. Department of Sociology and Anthropology, Auburn University.

1989 Seventeenth-Century Trade in the Colonial Southeast. *Southeastern Archaeology* 8:117–33.

1990 Historic Creek Architectural Adaptations to the Deerskin Trade. In *Archaeological Excavations at the Early Historic Creek Indian Town of Fusihatchee (Phase 1, 1988–1989)*, edited by Gregory Waselkov, John W. Cottier, and Craig Sheldon. Report submitted to the National Science Foundation, Grant BNS-8718934. On file, Laboratory of Archaeology, University of South Alabama, Mobile.

Waselkov, Gregory, and Kathryn Braund

1995 *William Bartram and the Southeastern Indians.* University of Nebraska Press, Lincoln.

Wauchope, Robert

1966 *Archaeological Survey of Northern Georgia with a Test of Some Cultural Hypotheses.* Memoir 21. Society for American Archaeology, Salt Lake City.

Webb, S. David, Jerald T. Milanich, Roger Alexon, and James S. Dunbar

1984 A Bison antiquus Kill Site, Wacissa River, Jefferson County, Florida. *American Antiquity* 49:384–92.

Webb, William S., and Charles Wilder
1952 *Archaeological Survey of Guntersville Basin.* University of Kentucky Press, Lexington.

Wenhold, Lucy
1936 *A 17th Century Letter of Gabriel Díaz Vara Calderón, Bishop of Cuba, Describing the Indians and Indian Missions of Florida.* Smithsonian Miscellaneous Collections 95 (16). Smithsonian Institution, Washington, D.C.

Williams, Mark
1994 Growth and Decline of the Oconee Province. In *The Forgotten Centuries: Indians and Europeans in the American South, 1521–1704,* edited by Charles Hudson and Carmen Chaves Tesser, 179–96. University of Georgia Press, Athens.

Wood, W. Dean, and R. Jerald Ledbetter
1990 *Rush: An Early Woodland Period Site in Northwest Georgia.* Occasional Papers in Cultural Resource Management No. 4. Georgia Department of Transportation, Atlanta.

Wright, J. Leitch
1986 *Creeks and Seminoles.* University of Nebraska Press, Lincoln.

Wynn, Jack
1990 *Mississippi Period Archaeology of the Georgia Blue Ridge Mountains.* Laboratory of Archaeology Series Report No. 27. University of Georgia, Athens.

Index

Bartram, William: on Coosa town, 71; on Creeks, 51–52, 53, 54, 62; on sociopolitical leaders, 58, 66; on tattooes, 68

Baxter site (9Go8): continued occupation of, 32; location of, 20; Poarch Farm site and, 28; as political center, 24–25

Bead Field site (1Ta208), 73

beads: abundance of, 44; Bell Field site, 26; Childersburg site, 70; Coats Bend site, 107; at Coosa River origins, 42; dating of, 99, 100–101; diverse use of, 68; Etowah site, 90; Little Egypt site, 90; Poarch Farm site, *pl.* 2; Sixtoe site, 22; as status symbols, 94; Talimico site, 83–84; Terrapin Creek site, 101; Weiss Reservoir cluster, 106, *pl.* 4; Whorton's Bend site, 112; Woods Island site, 115, *pl.* 7

beans, 4, 13. *See also* domesticated plants

Beauchamp, M. de, 75

Bell Field site: burials at, 26, 26, 27; comparisons to, 31–32; location of, 20; political authority at, 25, 28; structures at, 25–26

Beloved Old Men, 59

Benoît de St. Clair, Jean Baptiste, 74

Biedma, Luys, 34, 82

bison hunting, 110

black drink ceremony, 26, 65, 66

Blue Ridge Province, 5, 85

Bonar, William, 1757 map by, 71, 72, 74, 76, 79

Booker, Karen, 48

bows and arrows, 13, 63, 67

Bradford Ferry site: burials at, 106; location of, 103, 104; migration of, 109; structures at, 105

brass objects: abundance of, 44; Childersburg site, 70; dating of, 99–100; Little Egypt site, *pl.* 2; Weiss Reservoir cluster, 106, *pl.* 4; Whorton's Bend site, 112, *pl.* 5; Woods Island site, 115, *pl.* 8

Breed Town (or Camp), 76

Brown Farm site, 20, 32, 44

buildings: Bell Field site, 25–26; Hiwassee

Island Mound, 22; in typical capitals, 16–17; Upper Creek, 51–52, 53, 54; Weiss Reservoir cluster, 105. *See also* fortifications; housing

burials and burial goods: Bell Field site, 26, 26, 27; Childersburg site, 70; dating goods of, 99–100, 115; epidemics evident in, 97, 98; Etowah site, 28–29; King site, 84, 90, 91, 92, 98, 106, *pl.* 3; Little Egypt site, 31–32, 89–90; Sixtoe site, 22–23, 24; social rank evident in, 11–12, 15, 91, *pl.* 1; Talimico site, 83–84; Upper Creek religion and, 65; Weiss Reservoir cluster, 106–7, *pl.* 4; Whorton's Bend site, 110, 111, 112; Woodland period, 9–12; Woods Island site, 115–16

busk (Green Corn Ceremony), 64

Bussells Island, 35, 80

buttons, 115

Cahokia site, 95

Calderón, Gabriel Díaz Vara (bishop), 80, 96

Caldwell, Joseph, 19, 23

Carters cluster, 86, 100, 103

Cartersville Fault, 19, 85, 104. *See also* ecotone boundary

Cartersville (Ga.), sites near, 85, 86, 100, 103

Caskinampo people, 48

Caxiti (town), 40

Cayomulgi (town), 77

Chalahume (town), 48, 86, 87

Chalakagay (town), 77

Chartier, Peter, 77

Chattahoochee River, 60, 62

Chattanooga (Tenn.), sites near, 78, 85, 86

chenopodium, 8, 10–11. *See also* domesticated plants

Cherokee language, 48–49

Cherokees, 63, 66, 74, 116

Chiaha (chiefdom): Coosa influence on, 35, 47; language of, 48; location of, 2, 60, 62, 81, 86, 87

Chickasaw dialect, 49

Hally, David J.: on Bell Field site, 25; on demography, 33, 87; on Leake site, 88; on Little Egypt site, 31, 89; on Potts' Tract site, 32; on sixteenth-century sites, 85; on Sixtoe Mound site, 23, 24
Hansen, Asael T., 70
Hathagalgi moiety, 55, 60
Hawkins, Benjamin, 71, 73
healers, 65–66
heniha, 59
Hightower Village site, 40, 41
Hiwassee Island, 22, 23
Hiwassee River, 3–4, 86, 87
Hobohatchey (mico), 62, 74
Holstein, Harry O., 106
Homann map, 79
Hopewellian Interaction Sphere, 11
Horned Snake, 65
hospitality, 57
housing: King site, 18, 88, 114–15; Leake site, 18; Mississippian, 17–18; Sixtoe site, 24; Upper Creeks, 51–52, 53, 54; winter vs. summer, 17–18, 88; Woodland period, 9–10; Woods Island site, 114–15
Hudson, Charles: on Cofitachequi, 95; institutes by, xiii; linguistic affiliations and, 48; Pardo's route reconstructed by, 84; synthesis by, xi; on Talisi location, 117
human effigy pots, 26, 26, 27
hunting: changes in, 8–9, 13; importance of, 89; as men's task, 67; Milner Village site, 110; political hierarchy and, 59; preferences in, 55. See also agriculture
Hurley site, 103, 104, 105

ice age, 6–8
indirect historical approach, xiv
iron goods: dating of, 100; Hightower Village site, 40, 41; Weiss Reservoir cluster, 106; Whorton's Bend site, 110, 112; Woods Island site, 115, pl. 8
Itaba. See Ytaua/Itaba (town)

Jackson's Ford, 117
Johnstone Farm site, 40, 90
Jones, C. C., 42

Kawitas (emperor), 75
Kelly, Arthur R., 22, 23, 25, 32
Kerlérec, Louis Billouart de, 75
King site: artifacts from, 40, 88–89, 110, 112; burials at, 84, 90, 91, 92, 98, 106, pl. 3; dating of, 99; excavations at, 87–88; housing at, 18, 88, 114–15; location of, 20, 102
kinship, Mississippian period, 14–15. See also matrilineal system
Knight, Vernon, 14–15, 65, 77–78
knives/swords: Bell Field site, 26, 27; Childersburg site, 70; dating of, 99; Etowah site, 90, pl. 1; King site, 90, 91, pl. 3; Little Egypt site, 90; significance of, 15, 26; Sixtoe site, 22; Whorton's Bend site, 112; Woods Island site, 113, 115, pl. 7
knotweed, 10–11. See also domesticated plants
Koasati language, 48–49
Koasati people, 60, 62, 80, 114
Kymulga phase, 76, 77, 100, 117

labor, gendered division of, 66–67
Lamar period, 29, 32, 88, 101
Langford, James B.: on Bell Field site, 25; on demography, 33, 87; on sixteenth-century sites, 85; on Sixtoe Mound site, 23, 24
languages, 48–49
Larson, Lewis, 28–29, 31
Leake site, 18, 20, 88, pl. 2
Levasseur, Charles, 74, 79, 96
limestone, pottery tempered with, 23
Little Abihka (town), 73
Little Egypt phase, 31
Little Egypt site: artifacts from, pl. 2; burials at, 31–32, 89–90; de Soto at, 35, 37; excavations at, 87–88; founding of, 92; location of, 7, 20, 84–85, 102; political

Little Egypt site—*continued*
authority of, 1, 32; size of, 44; subsistence remains at, 89
Little Tennessee River: geography of, 3–4; sites along, 35, 85, *86, 87*
Logan Martin Lake, 112
Lookout Mountain, 104–5
Lower Creeks, 60, *61,* 62
Luna, Tristán de: Coosa described by, 1, 38, 85, 118; expedition of, xvii, 38, 39, 40–45, 78

maize. *See* corn (maize)
marriage, 56–57, 94. *See also* matrilineal system
Master of Breath, 64
matrilineal system: in inheritance, 14–15; in political organization, 58; in social organization, 54–57, *56*
matrilocal residence, 57
maygrass, 10–11. *See also* domesticated plants
McGillivray, Lachlan, 74
men: dress of, 67–68; labor tasks of, 67
menstruation, 66
metal artifacts, 94, 120. *See also* brass objects; iron goods
Milner Village site: artifacts from, *pl. 5–6;* burials at, 110, *111;* excavation of, 107, 109; food remains at, 110; location of, *108*
Mississippian period: Barnett phase in, 31–33; beginnings of, 19–20; Bell Field phase in, 25–26, 28; chiefs as divine in, 18–19; Etowah phase in, 22–25, 28–30; Little Egypt phase in, 31; overview of, 21; sites in, 20; sociopolitical structure in, 13–16; structures in, 16–18; Woodstock phase in, 19, 21–22
Mitchell map (1755), 76, 79
Mobile (Ala.), sites near, 40
Moccasin Bend (Tennessee River), 78
Mohman site, 40
moieties, 55–56, *56,* 60
Montalván, Alonso de, 40

Montgomery (Ala.), Spanish expedition at, 40
Moorehead, Warren K., 28, 31–32, 90
Mortier map, 79
mounds: Bell Field site, 25–26; at Coosa River origins, 42; decline of population and building of, 97, 99, 119; Etowah Culture, 22–23, 28; Little Egypt site, 31; Mississippian, 17; pyramid type of, 19; in typical capitals, 16–17. *See also* burials and burial goods; *specific sites*
Moundville site, 29, 95
Mouse Creek phase site, 18
Muskogean language, 48–49, 62, 114

Nairne, Thomas, 80, 113
Nanipacana (town), 38
Napier Culture, 12
Napochies: alliances of, 60; disappearance of, 78–79; language of, 49; location of, *2, 85, 86;* raid against, 44–45; tribute from, 94
Naroll, Raoul, 87
Natchez Indians, 19, 66, 76–77
National Endowment for the Humanities, xiii
Native Americans, removal of, 120–21
Neely Henry Reservoir sites, 107, *108,* 109–12
9Go5 site, 22
9Go9 site, 22

Ocmulgee River, 62
Oconee River, 62
Ocute Province, *2,* 35, 95
Okfuskee cluster, 50–51, 60, *61,* 74
Olamico. *See* Chiaha (chiefdom)
Onachiqui (town), 40
Ooe-asa (town), 76
Oostanaula River, 3–4
ornaments: description of, 67–68; Etowah site, 90, *pl. 1;* King site, 90, 92; significance of, 15; Sixtoe site, 22–23; Weiss Reservoir cluster, 106, *pl. 4;* Whorton's Bend site, 112;

rituals, 26, 64–66
rivers: in population movements, 101, 104; town locations and, 54; in transportation needs, 3–4
Rogan, John P., 28
Romans, Bernard: on burial goods, 65; on domesticated animals, 67; on dress, 68; on hospitality, 57; on town square function, 59; on warfare, 63
Rome (Ga.), sites near, 38, 40, 42, 80, 85, 86, 100
Rostlund, Erhard, 110
Roth, Janet, 89
Rush site, 10, 11

sabia (crystal), 65
Santa Elena (S.C.), settlement of, 45
Satapo (town), 2, 47, 48, 86, 87
Sauz, Mateo del, 38, 40, 42, 44, 85
Savannah River, 9
Schnell, Frank, 62
scissors, Woods Island site, 115
Scott, Susan, 110
Seale map, 79
Second Men, 59
Seven Springs site: artifacts from, 105, 106, 110, pl. 4; location of, 103, 104
Sharp-Breasted Snake, 65
Shawnee Indians, 77
Sheldon, Elisabeth, 70–71
shell middens, 9
sickle blades, 40, 41
silver, 68, 70
site 9Fl175, 40
site 9Mu104, 9, 10, 11
Sixtoe Mound site: burials at, 22–23, 24; location of, 20; occupation of, 32
slave trade, 113
Smith, Bruce, 12
soapstone, 5, 9
social inequality: decline of, 119; evidence of, 11–12, 15; hereditary leadership and, 14; in housing location, 17
sociopolitical organization: Archaic period, 8–9; Coosa decline and, 119–20;

Mississippian period, 13–16; Pleistocene period, 6–7; Upper Creek, 54–63, 56; warfare's role in, 63; Woodland period, 9–12
Soto, Hernando de: on chiefdoms and war, 15–16; Coosa's power and, 118; dating goods of, 100; expedition accounts of, 34–35, 36, 37–38; expedition's impact on Coosa, 43–44; reconstructing route of, xvii, 1, 79, 82–83, 84
Spanish explorers: dating goods of, 99–100; Indian response to, 43; material culture of, 83–84; in raid against Napochies, 44–45. See also specific explorers
squash, 4, 8, 13. See also domesticated plants
stone image, pl. 1
stone pipes, 106–7, pl. 6
stone tools: European goods vs. access to, 104; King site, 91; location of, 5; replacement of, 120; Weiss Reservoir cluster, 106–7; Whorton's Bend site, 112, pl. 6. See also projectile points
subsistence. See agriculture; food remains; hunting
Summer Institute on Southeastern Indians and Spanish Explorers, xiii
Summerour Mound, 19, 20
sumpweed, 8, 10–11. See also domesticated plants
sunflowers, 4, 8, 10–11. See also domesticated plants
Swancy site, 20, 32
Swanton, John: on Abihka defeat, 116; on Abihkutci, 74; on Breed Town (or Camp), 76; on Creek Confederacy, 63; on Okfushee and Coosa peoples, 60; on refugee Shawnee, 77; de Soto's route reconstructed by, 82–83; on Tuskigee location, 79
Sylacauga Water Works site, 54, 77

Taitt, David, 71, 76–77, 79
Talimachusy (town), 78
Talimico (town), 83–84

Marvin T. Smith is professor of anthropology at Valdosta State University. He is the author of *Archaeology of Aboriginal Culture Change in the Interior Southeast* (UPF, 1987) and numerous other monographs and articles.

Ripley P. Bullen Series
Florida Museum of Natural History
Edited by Jerald T. Milanich